Core Principles of Meditation for Therapy

Core Principles of
Meditation for Therapy

Improving the Outcomes for
Psychotherapeutic Treatments

Annellen M. Simpkins
C. Alexander Simpkins

WILEY

Published by John Wiley & Sons, Inc., Hoboken, New Jersey.
Published simultaneously in Canada.

This publication is designed to provide accurate and authoritative information in regard to the subject matter covered. It is sold with the understanding that the publisher is not engaged in rendering professional services. If legal, accounting, medical, psychological or any other expert assistance is required, the services of a competent professional should be sought.

For general information on our other products and services, please contact our Customer Care Department within the U.S. at 800-956-7739, outside the U.S. at 317-572-3986, or fax 317-572-4002.

Wiley publishes in a variety of print and electronic formats and by print-on-demand. Some material included with standard print versions of this book may not be included in e-books or in print-on-demand. If this book refers to media such as a CD or DVD that is not included in the version you purchased, you may download this material at http://booksupport.wiley.com. For more information about Wiley products, visit www.wiley.com.

Library of Congress Cataloging-in-Publication Data is Available

ISBN 978-1-118-68959-2 (paperback)
ISBN 978-1-118-82917-2 (ePDF)
ISBN 978-1-118-82915-8 (epub)
ISBN 978-1-119-17169-0 (obk)

Cover design: Wiley
Cover image: © iStockphoto/Yuri

Printed in the United States of America

FIRST EDITION

PB Printing   10 9 8 7 6 5 4 3 2 1

We dedicate Core Principles of Meditation *to our wonderful children, Alura Louise Aguilera and Charles Alexander Simpkins, who both grew up with meditation long before its time, and trusted us to embrace these practices. Now as successful professionals in their own fields, they continue to use meditation in positive ways, as they witness it coming into its own. We also dedicate this work to their loving spouses, Anthony Aguilera and Kyongmi Simpkins, and to our beautiful grandchildren, Kira Aguilera and Kaia Aguilera.*

Contents

Introduction

The psychotherapy world is excited about meditation and mindfulness. Many therapists are becoming enthusiastic to try it and wonder how to use it in therapy with clients. Research supports this enthusiasm. Studies show that meditation can improve outcomes with many psychological disorders because of the way it changes the brain. For example, many researchers have found that meditating increases feelings of well-being and happiness. These are qualities that most clients are seeking from therapy. Meditation also enhances emotional and self-regulation, abilities that psychotherapy strives to foster. In addition, meditation helps practitioners to be both calm and alert, thereby facilitating achievement in life without anxiety and stress. And efficacy research described throughout the book shows that outcomes are improved by adding meditation into therapy. Thus, there is scientific evidence that the very qualities which meditation develops are particularly well suited to enhance your psychotherapy, blending well with methods that you are already doing with your clients.

ABOUT THIS PACKAGE

This book/DVD/CD package gives you the tools you need to bring many meditation methods, including mindfulness, into your psychotherapy

work with clients. You can access these resources at www.wiley.com/go/
meditation3e. We created it in multiple media to help make the experience
more vivid and learnable. After all, meditation is an *experience*. If you are
planning to use it with clients, you must first experience it for yourself. By
providing varied media, our hope is that you will get your own felt sense
along with a clear understanding of what meditation is and how it can help,
as you also learn a wide variety of meditative techniques to use in your
therapy work.

About the Book

The book is divided into 20 chapters, each illustrating a core principle of
meditation. Most chapters include exercises. We have written the exercise
as if speaking to a client. You can use the text directly as a script to read to
your client, but we suggest that as you become more familiar with therapeutic meditation, you vary the scripts to suit the unique individuality of your
client. Also, be yourself! You will develop your own ways of introducing
meditation and applying it that fit your therapeutic style and personality.
Sincerity is one of the hallmarks of good therapist. Be the great therapist
that you already are, who now is adding meditation to your therapeutic
approaches.

In Part I, you will learn about the rich philosophical background from
which meditation and mindfulness spring. Not only are the traditions fascinating and beautiful, they also offer ways to look at reality through a different
lens. These unique perspectives turn some of our commonly held assumptions upside down. From a different point of view, new solutions emerge.

Part II provides the neuroscience of meditation for your understanding.
There are distinct ways that meditation changes the brain and nervous system, and these alterations can be a corrective for nervous system patterns
found in psychological problems. Neuroscience also shows that there are different types of meditation, so you don't have to use the same meditation for
every client and every situation. Throughout this package, you will be guided
in when to use the various types for working with different psychological
problems.

Part III provides tools for learning meditation. People sometimes fear
that meditation is a strange and foreign practice that is far beyond them.

But in truth, meditation draws on our everyday capacities to pay attention, to sense, and to move. This section offers exercises that will make it easy to begin meditating.

Part IV gives meditation instructions for three main types of meditation: focus meditation, which involves keeping attention steady; open-focus mindfulness meditation, during which attention is allowed to drift from target to target, and no-focus meditation, which clears the mind and lets attention be.

Finally in Part V, we show you how to apply meditation with clients. People who suffer with psychological problems are often unhappy and despair of ever feeling different, but meditation research on compassion and gratitude shows that happiness can be developed. This section begins with instructions on how to help your clients to have the experience of well-being. We also guide in how to integrate meditation into your practice, answering many of the commonly asked nuts and bolts questions. Chapters 13 to 19 offer techniques and protocols for common psychological problems of stress, emotional regulation, depression, bipolar disorder, anxiety, trauma, and substance abuse. The Conclusion chapter illustrates the core principle of meditation, which you can cultivate to make your life what you want it to be by meditating.

About the Videos

The videos support the content of the book to clarify, fill out, and add to your experience. We talk directly to you, the therapist, and invite you to share in many different learning experiences. You may also want to share these videos with your clients.

In Video 1, you will gain a clear sense of how the philosophy of the East and the philosophy of the West can integrate together to give you a broader paradigm for understanding your clients and the world. Video 2 explains the neuroscience of meditation. Some people will become more receptive to meditating when they understand how it changes their brain in healing ways. This video provides easy to understand explanations so that you can share this information with any client. Video 3 gives exercises you can use to train attention, sensory awareness, and body movement. These exercises prepare you and your clients to meditate. They build skills that will give your client a natural and easy transition into meditation. Videos 4, 5, and 6 teach the different forms of meditation with exercises you can follow easily. Video 7 guides in compassion and gratitude meditations, which are extremely helpful for clients who are hard on themselves and others and often miss the goodness around them. Video 8 offers useful tips for integrating meditation into your practice.

We encourage you to join in with the videos and experience each form of meditation for yourself, to give you a broad range of tools for working with the unique individuality of your client.

About the Audios

The audio recordings offer instructions that can be given directly to clients to guide them during or between sessions or that you can use to develop your own meditation skills. Audio 1 trains the tools of meditation for enhancing attention, sensing, and body awareness. Audio 2 instructs in focus meditation by holding attention on one thing. Audio 3 provides mindfulness instructions, allowing the focus of attention to move nonjudgmentally, with the flow of consciousness, moment by moment. Audio 4 brings the listener to a clear mind through visualizing an image. Audio 5 gives a guided compassion meditation.

CONCLUSION

Clients are often surprised that they can create a quiet moment of peace, or discover that they have the ability to focus when they choose, or learn that they can be aware of their experiencing moment by moment. They become more hopeful and open as they learn to forgive themselves and others, compassionately, and accept difficult situations and people. Then they can appreciate the beauty and goodness in the world that they have been missing.

We have used all of the forms of meditation and each of the techniques with clients over many years and seen them grow and develop as they bring meditation into their lives. Our hope is that you will find meditation to be a resource for yourself and your clients, as we have. We invite you to walk the meditative path. Enjoy the journey!

Core Principles of Meditation for Therapy

PART I
THEORETICAL FOUNDATIONS

1

Return to Emptiness

Core Principle 1: Learn from What Is and What Is Not.

Wisdom alone is a science of other sciences, and of itself.
—***Plato*, The Dialogues of Plato**

It is the readiness of the mind that is wisdom.
—**Shunryu Suzuki, Soto Zen master**

INTRODUCTION

The search for wisdom has motivated human beings to learn about the external world and the inner self. It lies at the root of Western science and Eastern mysticism. And yet each perspective is based on very different foundations, taken for granted, about the nature of reality. Psychotherapists gain much by considering both East and West.

Through scientific inquiry in the West, many great discoveries and understandings about the world have led to amazing technologies, improving people's quality of life. We can now relate person to person across the globe with just a few keystrokes. Healing has been improved as well, with medications that can stimulate and rebalance neurotransmitters, so vital to health. And psychotherapy has advanced with cognitive-behavioral and dynamic therapies, which harness the power of reason for regulating emotions and directing behavior. We use scientific efficacy to help guide us to use the best treatments we can. The assumptions we take in the West lead us in certain directions, defining our options and bringing expected results. The foundations go all the way back to ancient times in Greece, where first principles of science were just beginning to be uncovered.

But now we know that the wisdom of the East also has valuable tools for psychotherapy and for deepening our understanding of the nature of reality itself. Eastern wisdom is based on different foundations from Western ones. Formulated by ancient gurus and spiritual leaders, these foundations led to unique mental and physical disciplines of meditation, quite distinct from the rigors of science. And yet, similar to the science of the West, meditation provides a way to investigate the outer world and know the inner self. Meditation includes varied and highly refined practices, developed over thousands of years. Through engagement with these practices, problems clear away for a healthy flow of mental and physical energy. These Eastern practices lead to improved health, both mental and physical, opening new perspectives that are helpful for therapy. By combining the wisdom from both East and West, creative therapeutic alternatives emerge.

This chapter weaves the science from the West with the wisdom from East to form a new integration. A healing network of new potentials unfolds when there is an understanding of both types of wisdom.

FOUNDATIONS OF WESTERN SCIENCE

The object of knowledge is what exists and its function to know about reality.

—Plato

The ancients of the West looked up into the heavens, and they saw material substance—planets, stars, sun, and moon. And when they looked down, they saw earth, water, and trees. They wondered how to know about the things that can be observed and use them to enhance the quality of their lives. Their curiosity led to science as a way to understand the composition and nature of this material substance they observed all around them. They used the scientific method to explore their world and enhance the quality of life.

First Principles

Science revealed that this world of material things has a rational order. The ancients of the West sought to uncover this order by thoughtful inquiry. They believed that the order must have come from first principles and sought to discover these principles by using reasoning.

Early pre-Socratics proposed various first principles. Thales (625–545 BCE) thought that water was the first principle and that the earth could be stable because it rested in water. Anaximander (610–540 BCE) saw four elements as the fundamental building blocks for all that exists in the world, which he and other Greeks identified as earth, air, fire, and water.

Others proposed that the exact material of the universe was not the key to understanding the principles. First they sought to understand the ways by which material substance undergoes change. Heraclitus (d. 500 BCE) believed that everything is in a continual state of flux. You don't step into the same river twice, because the water always flows. Everything is continually undergoing change. Therefore, change is the very essence of material substance.

By contrast, Parmenides (540–515 BCE) postulated that everything is one and nothing changes. His reason was that if everything changes, some things come into being and exist while others go out of being and are not. But how can we talk about something that is not? We can't; it is impossible to know something that doesn't exist. Therefore, change is unreal.

Democritus (460–370 BCE) believed that change could be explained in a different way, by the interaction among tiny, indivisible particles he called atoms. These atoms exist in space, the void, and make up the material substances we see around us. Our senses can't detect these tiny particles, but through the varied combinations of atoms, we get our rich and diverse, ever-changing world. Modern science builds on this original insight, developing sophisticated understandings through advances in technology that allow us to explore more deeply. We now know that there are smaller particles than atoms. Particle physics researchers today are still searching for the smallest unit, from which everything else derives.

Progress of the Scientific Method

As science became more sophisticated, the ancients of the West noticed how much their senses misled them. The essence of material substance that appears to us is hidden. The deeper, true nature of substance is not directly accessible to our senses. The great philosopher Plato (428–348 BCE) believed that the use of reason, not the senses, was the better way to understand the deeper nature of reality. He developed a dialectical method, expressed through the words of his teacher Socrates (470–360 BCE), that used careful questioning through hypothesis. These methods of reasoning led to the scientific methods used today. Many modern forms of therapy still use Socratic questioning as a means to guiding clients to deeper truth about themselves.

Aristotle (384–322 BCE) developed this form of reasoning further. Since something is definitely there, we must understand its causes. Aristotle introduced a theory of causality itself with his famous four causes (2008, ii 3, 8), which forms the bedrock for Western science. The *material cause* accounts for what things are made of. The *efficient cause* is the force or agent that brings them about. The *formal cause* is the ordered state that the change produces, and the *final cause* is the goal toward which the change is directed. He applied this theory of causality to things in the world. For example, think of a beautifully crafted box. The material cause is the wood it is made of. The efficient cause is the craftsperson who created it. The formal cause is the sketch or plan the artisan used to help direct the box's design, and the final cause is the reason for creating the box, perhaps as a gift for someone.

This way of thinking influences the approach to psychotherapeutic treatments today. We think about the material causes when we look at the underlying biological condition. We analyze the conditions that may have led to the disorder, the formal causes in the behaviors and actions involved, and the final cause as underlying motivations. Fundamental is the assumption that something is there—a disorder, a problem—and through the use of objective, scientific methods, we can uncover its causes to help cure it.

Since there is a real world, psychological problems should be viewed as tangible entities. We must identify the problem, define its fundamental elements, and analyze its causes. Only then can we devise ways to treat the problem. Thus, we have diagnoses to identify psychological problems and protocols for curing them. Through the years of research and practice, these methods have grown more sensitive and helpful.

FOUNDATIONS OF EASTERN WISDOM

When your spirit is not in the least clouded, when the clouds of bewilderment clear away, there is the true void.
—*Miyamoto Musashi,* The Book of Five Rings

The ancients of the East looked up into the heavens, and they saw a vast emptiness. Although they could point to planets and stars in the sky, they noticed that the heavenly bodies moved and disappeared. They observed that all living things on earth were transitory, coming into being and then passing away. Everything changed in cycles. They saw that the seasons rotated around every year, and day continually turned into night and back to day. They studied the nature of different kinds of change and recorded their understandings in the now-famous book, the *I Ching, The Book of Changes.* They came to recognize that what was most fundamental and true about the universe was that in its deeper nature, it is empty.

The Unreality of Appearances

According to Eastern wisdom, the conditions of the physical world and the senses may give an appearance of an apparent object, but no object actually is present. Reality is like a mirage of water on an expanse of sunny highway. No water is there, merely its realistic appearance, due to light bending on the hot road. Similarly, the world that we experience is a function of perceptual conditions. Consciousness makes it seem to exist.

Perceptions of the world are relative because they rely on external criteria, standards that are limited by our perspective. For example, the perception of distance in space is relative to our own capacities and size. The tiny ant cannot imagine crawling to a distant mountain. To an eagle, the same mountain peak may be close, a place for home.

The mushroom of a morning does not know (what takes place between) the beginning and end of a month; the short-lived cicada does not know (what takes place between) spring and autumn. These are instances of a short life. In the south of Khu there is the (tree) called Mind-ling, whose spring is 500 years and its autumn the same.
—The philosopher Chuang-tzu, quoted in Legge (1962, p. 166).

Foundation in the Tao

There is an empty ultimate reality underlying all that we see in the world. Without recognizing emptiness, we will never understand the true nature of the cosmos. For example, what makes a cup what it is? The answer is: the empty space within. Once you fill the cup with water, it can no longer be used for anything else but a container. In order to use the cup as a cup, you must empty it. The nature of a cup is in its emptiness, as is the universe in its deepest nature.

The ancients of the East called this emptiness Tao. All life follows Tao. Tao precedes and all else succeeds. As stated in the *Tao Te Ching*: "It [Tao] is bottomless, perhaps the ancestor of all things" (Chan, 1963, p. 141).

The Empty Tao

We are accustomed to defining emptiness as a state, a vacuum consisting of the absence of molecules. But from the Eastern perspective, emptiness, the Tao, is not simply a nothing, like a vacuum. Rather, it is the potential for everything. Tao is the source for potential from which all things emerge. The founder of Gestalt therapy, Fritz Perls (1969), noted that emptiness implies *no*-thingness, only process.

In our culture "nothingness" has a different meaning than it has in the Eastern religions. When we say "nothingness," there is a void, an emptiness, something deathlike. When the Eastern person says "nothingness," he calls it *no thingness*—there are no *things* there. There is only process, happening. . . . And we find when we accept and enter this nothingness, the void, then the desert starts to bloom. . . . The sterile void becomes the fertile void. (p. 57)

Thus, in the void, we find a source for creativity and therapeutic change. Devoid of problems, before they were formed, we can discover health and well-being.

Meditation: The Method for Attuning to Tao

How can we know this empty nature of the world? Understanding the nature of the universe does not involve the accumulation of new knowledge and information, nor does it engage rational thought. To truly understand emptiness, enter the *Way*, a process whereby you become empty yourself. The ancients of the East developed methods of meditation to become empty like the universe. By letting go of the objects of perception, you remove obstructions. You allow the flow of pure consciousness itself, and then you can know the world as it truly is.

> Make your will one! Don't listen with your ears, listen with your mind. No, don't listen with your mind, but listen with your spirit. Listening stops with the ears, the mind stops with recognition, but spirit is empty and waits on all things. The Way gathers in emptiness alone. Emptiness is the fasting of the mind.
> —The Taoist sage Chuang-tzu, quoted in Watson (1968, p. 58).

The Value of Emptiness

Long ago, there was a monk who had become famous for his skills at gardening. The king heard of his abilities and had him brought to his castle to plant a new garden. The monk agreed to do so if the king promised to follow his instructions. The king agreed. The monk asked that certain supplies be brought to the area. Then he told the king and his men to leave him alone. When the king and his men left, the monk sat down in the middle of the plot of land and began to meditate.

A few hours later, one of the king's men peeked in and saw the monk still meditating. Later that night, the king's men looked again, but the monk was still meditating. Food was brought to the monk the

(continued)

(*continued*)

following day, but he continued to meditate. Day after day passed in this way. The king began to feel impatient. Finally he could wait no longer. The king walked up to the meditating monk and said angrily, "I brought you here to create a beautiful garden, but all you have done for the past week is sit there!"

The monk said nothing and continued to meditate. Not being accustomed to being ignored, the king said fiercely, "I give you one more day to finish the task, and then I will kill you!"

The next day, the king marched into the garden space with his executioner carrying his sword. But what he found there took him completely by surprise. Stretching out before him was the most beautiful garden he had ever seen.

"How is it," asked the king, "that you sat for an entire week, doing nothing, and then created this most exquisite garden in only one day?"

The monk replied in a quiet, calm voice, "You asked me to create a beautiful garden, but to do so I must first become empty like nature. Then the rest is easy."

Meditation is a time to sit quietly. When you meditate, you take a break from all the usual thoughts and activities that fill your life. Then, in those moments of quiet, you begin to perceive clearly in a new way. You become in touch with silence within. We are all endowed with a mind that is clear, pure, and deep. This is what the Zen masters call our true nature. It is already there within, but we usually don't notice because we are too busy being pushed and pulled by our thoughts and desires.

Meditation is a tool that can teach us how to return to deeper experience to perceive clearly, resulting in a profound sense of calm and confidence that won't be shaken. This source within is valuable for mental health. As you get more accustomed to meditation, you realize that what seemed at first to be a nonactivity is its own kind of activity. Meditation gets us in touch with the source for well-being. By letting go and simply observing whatever occurs, you gain control.

The purpose is to see things as they are, to observe things as they are, and to let everything go as it goes. This is to put everything under control in its widest sense.

—Shunryu Suzuki, *Zen Mind, Beginner Mind*

Koans which are paradoxical questions to be solved without the use of reason, sitting in meditation, and other practices allow you to let go of the inner turmoil. You set aside your conceptualizing, objectifying rational thought, which creates the reality we see around us. In the empty moment, peaceful clarity is found.

Integration East and West

Thousands of years have passed since those early discoveries, both East and West. Today, thanks to verification from careful scientific research, the field of psychotherapy has come to recognize the value of meditation for psychological healing. Many have sought to integrate the Eastern meditative practices into treatments. But how can we integrate these meditative practices, which rest on opposite foundations from Western science? Can we reconcile these seemingly contradictory traditions? In this book/CD/DVD package, we offer an integration that allows the wisdom from the East to fit seamlessly with the science of the West, leading to a more comprehensive foundation from which to draw techniques for therapy.

Form Is Emptiness and Emptiness Is Form

In the Zen monastery, practitioners chant, "Form is emptiness and emptiness is form." One metaphor that may be helpful for understanding this relationship is to think of a mirror and its reflection. If emptiness is the mirror, substance (form) is the reflections. Reflections depend on a mirror to reflect them, but they aren't literally the mirror itself. And no matter what is reflected or how much the reflections may change, mirrors never change in what they are in themselves. The true nature of form is emptiness because emptiness is like mind's mirror that reflects forms, creating them in the interaction. They are inseparable, a unity.

Unity

As therapists, we recognize unity when we view our clients within their family context. There is no self outside of the environment because we are all part of our surrounding environment, just as our environment is part of us. Attachment theory shows how a lifetime of relationships evolves out of early interactions with the primary caregiver.

The Buddhist monk Fa-tsang (643–712) gave a demonstration of the unity to the empress Wu of China, who was studying Buddhism under him. He covered the entire floor, walls, and ceiling of a room in the palace with mirrors. Then he placed a statue of Buddha with a torch in the center. The moment the torch was lit, the empress saw infinite Buddhas all at once, each reflecting all the others. This image gave her a powerful experience of unity. Everything came into being at a single moment, existing together just as it was. After she saw this demonstration, the empress felt a deep understanding of what her teacher was trying to communicate.

Experience Integration with Indra's Net

Indra's net is a metaphor used to illustrate the emptiness and the interpenetration of all things in Buddhist philosophy. To begin this integrative journey, we invite you to have an image. Imagine a vast net that spreads infinitely in every direction with no beginning and no end. At each juncture of the net is a perfectly reflecting crystal-clear jewel. We are all jewels in this limitless net. If the net moves in one area, the movement ripples through the entire net, like a pebble thrown into a still pond. The net is a self-creating, self-sustaining network of interacting links. Hold this image in mind for a moment.

Now we turn to the recent discovery of neural networks. These networks are composed of on-off units, modeled as a simplified version of a neuron, known as a *perceptron*. Combined, these perceptrons form a network of interactions, which feed back and feed forward to form a network of interaction. These networks can be created to produce what resembles cognitive thought. They can be trained to learn how to recognize faces, distinguish dogs from cats, and perform other cognitive activities.

We are all involved in neural networks without realizing it. Consider when you use your credit card. Credit card companies have neural networks.

As you use your card, the information is fed into the network as it learns your typical patterns. Then, one day, perhaps you are on vacation in a new place or you make a larger purchase than usual, and you get a telephone call. "Did you make this purchase?" asks the network. Hopefully you answer yes, and the voice says, "Then I will authorize this purchase." The information is then fed back into the network, which has learned something new about your spending. With neural networks becoming more sophisticated, they eventually will be able to carry out more complex mental processes.

Of course, we know that each person is unique and separate, but from another perspective, we can see how much we are influenced by significant others. We are all part of a unity, which helps to shape what we become. And yet, at the same time, we are uniquely ourselves, with the choice of how to respond to that unity.

CONCLUSION

Now, with all this in mind, let's expand on Aristotle's assumption that either a thing is or is not. The great Buddhist philosopher Nagarjuna (150–250 BCE) said that a thing is, is not, neither and both. Particle physics has come to a similar conclusion, recognizing that at the microscopic level, we can't determine whether the substance of a particle is matter or energy. It seems to be neither and both. For psychotherapy, we gain from a broader, more open perspective. By holding the seemingly opposite worldviews from East and West together in a network, like a neural net, we gain a more inclusive point of view that produces new potentials. Drawing on emptiness and substance, more interventions become possible. We can better accommodate the unique individuality of each client and address the complexities of personality in each unique situation. May you hold Indra's net in mind as you work your way through this book, to incorporate new potentials for healing and well-being.

2

The Changing Self

Core Principle 2: Attune to the Natural Flow of Change.

All that we are, is the result of what we have thought: It is founded on our thoughts, it is made up of our thoughts.

—The Buddha, Dhammapada

Indeed, it is now clear that constant remodeling is one of the brain's defining features. Just as important is the now abundant evidence that the relationship between changes in the brain and changes in behavior is bidirectional: experience also can alter neural structure. This plasticity is a feature of the nervous system that persists throughout life, from embryonic development until old age.

—S. M. Breedlove, R. M. Rosenzweig, & N. V. Watson, Biological Psychology

INTRODUCTION

People usually believe in the reality of things. We take for granted that the world we perceive today will be here tomorrow. This natural assumption of constancy is often applied to our sense of self as well. We tend to believe that the way we have been in the past has a strong relationship to how we will be in the future. The new findings in neuroscience show that our brain is changing all through life. But meditation philosophies have long understood that the self is not quite what we think. Our experience of constancy is merely a taken-for-granted assumption that limits our possibilities. In fact, expecting constancy can be a barrier to new and creative possibilities. By recognizing our changing nature in mind and brain, we can free ourselves from this limitation and take an important step on the path to therapeutic change.

CHANGE IS IN THE NATURE OF THE BRAIN

The brain undergoes change all through life, and meditation is a method to activate positive brain change. This process of brain change occurs through neuroplasticity and neurogenesis. Neuroplasticity is the ability of the brain to reorganize its neural connections, structures, and pathways. Neurogenesis entails the growth of neurons all through life. For example, the area involved in learning and memory, the hippocampus, shrinks from trauma but grows new neurons following enriching experiences such as psychotherapy. These changes occur rapidly during brain development in utero and in early childhood, but continue to occur at every phase of life, even into old age (Gage, Eriksson, Perfilieva, & Bjork-Eriksson, 1998).

Brain Change through Development

The process of human development is one of the most dramatic examples of neurogenesis and neuroplasticity. Consider the amazing fact that we all begin as one single cell, the fertilized egg, that grows and matures into the adult, with a complex functioning brain composed of an estimated 86 billion neurons, each with hundreds of interconnections.

A New Look at the Nature versus Nurture Debate

The old debate between nature and nurture can now be viewed as an ongoing interaction between the two. Brain development is a continual exchange between inborn genetics and environmental influences, beginning from conception and continuing all through the developmental process. As therapists, we are aware of both influences and work with them sensitively to best help our clients make changes.

Childhood is a time when the brain is developing key skills that will be used throughout life. Anyone who has had contact with young children knows how open and curious toddlers can be. In fact, a toddler's brain is two times more active than an adult's brain. Although the infant brain contains most of the cells the infant has before birth, connections are forming and re-forming all through childhood. The interplay of genetics (nature) and environmental influences (nurture) is an ongoing influence on how the child will develop.

Everyone is born with a genetic constitution, called the *genome* or *genotype*. This genotype is the individual's genetic makeup. Genotype is distinguished from phenotype. The phenotype results from interplay between the genotype and the environment. Thus, the phenotype contains all the physical characteristics of the individual that result from certain environmental conditions. Although the genotype is determined at the moment of fertilization, the phenotype changes throughout life. The continual interaction between the genotype and experiences bring about these changes (Rossi, 2002). Studies of genetically identical mice raised by different mothers showed significant differences in behavior, particularly in their ability to learn and respond to stress (Francis, Szegda, Campbell, Martin, & Insel, 2003). All of these studies can serve as a beacon of hope for the potential power of psychotherapy when it fosters new experiences for clients.

Sensitive and Critical Periods

Synaptic patterns can change throughout life, but there are certain times in early development when the nervous system is even more capable of changing in response to experience. Critical periods are time-limited windows of opportunity. At these times, neuronal pathways await specific information from experience in order to trigger genetics for normal development. If the brain does not receive the appropriate stimulus, certain skills become more difficult or even impossible to acquire later. Sensitive periods last longer than critical periods. During these times, the nervous system is more receptive to certain environmental stimuli for learning.

Certain skills are attained during the critical periods of childhood. During the first years of life, the window of opportunity is wide open for visual and auditory development. The ability to use both eyes together—binocular vision—occurs during a critical period between 3 and 8 months. Motor skills have a critical period during the first year of life, although there is quite a bit of variability on when the infant performs any motor skills, such as sitting up, crawling, and walking.

Language development is ongoing for the first 10 years of life. But the critical period that sets the stage for language ability takes place during the first few years. Thus, when parents talk to their infant, they are providing the stimuli the infant's brain needs to be able to develop the language centers. All of these critical and sensitive periods have more plasticity than was previously believed possible. Many of the meditative practices taught in this book can help to correct deficits in these primary skills of vision, movement, and language.

One of the crucial critical periods for healthy emotional development is forming attachments to primary caregivers. Our social interactions, especially with those who are closest to us early in life, have an enduring effect on our brain development. Parental imprinting takes place prenatally and continues during the first 18 months of a child's life. These early relationship experiences can continue to influence emotions, thoughts, and behavior ever after. If a child is subjected to stress prenatally or separation from the caregiver during infancy, he or she will have a tendency to increased anxiety later in life (Meaney, 2001). However, a low-stress pregnancy and nurturing early years with affection and love provides protection against later anxiety (Vallée et al., 1997). Although these early attachment experiences are formative, they have been shown to have some neuroplasticity and neurogenesis. For example, the hippocampus may develop smaller as a result of trauma in early childhood. But research shows that meditation and other therapy methods that help overcome these developmental problems result in a growth in the hippocampus, due to neurogenesis (Kheirbek & Hen, 2011). Meditation can successfully alter attachment problems that may have occurred early in life by bringing about corrective emotional experiences.

CHANGE IN THE ADOLESCENT BRAIN

Adolescence is a time for dramatic brain changes, and meditation can help make these changes flow better. New understanding of how the brain undergoes change during adolescence may help us understand just why adolescent clients may be impulsive, may take risks, and may make poor decisions.

The brain reaches its peak weight by around 10 to 12 years of age, but it will undergo a great deal of change before it reaches maturity. During early development, the brain undergoes pruning, where synaptic connections and cells that are not being used die to make room for new cells and connections. A pruning process also occurs during adolescence, when close to half of the synaptic connections are eliminated (Spear, 2010). Typically, we think that neuroplasticity means adding new connections, and often it does.

Researchers believe that the refining of synaptic connections in adolescence makes space for mature patterns to form (Zehr, Todd, Schultz, McCarthy, & Sisk, 2006).

In general, the adolescent's brain becomes more efficient and streamlined. Less energy is required for each region to function well, and blood flow declines (Spear, 2010). But we see an order in these changes, which might account for why adolescents are impulsive. The changes occur first in the posterior (back) areas of the sensory and motor cortex. The result is that adolescents often develop sensory and motor skills, expressed in artistic talent and athletic ability. But anterior (front) parts of the frontal cortex develop much later. Here is where judgment and executive functions are performed. In addition, adolescents tend to feel their emotions more intensely than adults, and the shifts in hormones that occur during adolescence helps to account for this emotional intensity. Adolescents are exposed to higher levels of stress hormones than adults, and the stressful events in their lives, such as academics and social pressures, increase activation of the hypothalamus–pituitary–adrenal (HPA) fear/stress pathway. The HPA pathway prepares the body for action when under threat and then returns the system to a lower activation when the threat has passed.

But if the HPA pathway remains activated over time, it becomes a stress pathway, where the nervous system is chronically overactivated. Adolescents are often experiencing chronic stress reactions, making self-regulation more difficult.

Some of the key tasks of adolescence may be to learn how to regulate emotions and make good decisions, even when emotionally aroused. Mature adults can regulate stress successfully and be more responsive to their nervous system signals. But for adolescents, emotional regulation is an ongoing challenge. Adolescence is a time of experimentation and learning that, in the best cases, will lead to a fully functioning adult brain.

BRAIN CHANGE FROM EXPERIENCE

Neuroplasticity also manifests in a way that is important for psychotherapy, when it occurs in response to experience. Experience-based neuroplasticity can happen all through life and in varied circumstances. It can be positive and expanding from experiences like meditation, or negative and constricting from trauma and stress. We see negative neuroplasticity associated with stress found in many psychological disorders, including posttraumatic stress disorder, major depression, and borderline personality disorder (Sala et al., 2004). People suffering from these problems show atrophy in their hippocampus. Psychotherapy can help to reverse this adverse effect. The hippocampus can undergo positive neuroplasticity, becoming larger than normal. An interesting study of London taxi cab drivers found that they had larger-than-normal hippocampi as compared to bus drivers (Maguire et al., 2000). The explanation is that cab drivers spend more time navigating to new locations. One of the functions of the hippocampus is correlated with finding our location in space.

Other studies have found that hippocampal growth can be stimulated to enhance functioning. In one study, seniors were trained to juggle three balls. Measurements on functional magnetic resonance imaging found increases in gray matter relating to skill acquisition as well as increases in the nucleus accumbens (part of the dopamine system) and the hippocampus (Boyke, Driemeyer, Gaser, Buchel, & May, 2008). Growth is often correlated with improved functioning, just as shrinking is associated with declines. Whenever we can stimulate new growth, we are more likely to help our clients improve their functioning.

PERCEPTION CREATES OUR SENSE OF CONSTANCY

With our brain undergoing so much change over our lifespan, why does our sense of self and the world seem so lasting? The illusion of a constant, unchanging reality is the result of how our brain processes information. Consciousness is constructed from the stimuli around us combined with the mind and brain's capacity to make sense of what is perceived. A good example of how we construct a meaningful sense of things is illustrated by the illusion shown in Figure 2.1. As you look at this picture, do you see a triangle? The triangle is very compelling, and most people will see a triangle there. But actually there is no triangle, only three Pacmen. The brain constructs the image of the triangle from the cues it receives.

Figure 2.1   Pacmen Triangle Illusion

Similarly, when we listen to a series of varying tones over time, we hear a melody. The temporal lobes process the sound to give us a flow of notes heard together. Another example is movies. Our occipital lobes process visual stimuli so that when we are watching a varying series of pictures flickering at a certain range or speed, we see coherent action: a moving picture. The mind and brain put the separate pictures together to give us a unity, and its constancy is experienced as a reality. Thus, the movie we see is our mind-brain consciousness, constructing meaningful enduring experience.

PERCEIVING CHANGE FOR THERAPY

This ability to construct a reality from cues in the environment has a significant application to psychotherapy. By getting in touch with this process, clients can become aware of how their problems, which feel so intractable, are not, in their deeper nature as a unique human being, fixed and lasting. We have heard many of our clients tell us they are a depressed, anxious, or addicted person who will never change. They have no idea that their problem is the result of a mind-brain adjustment, which links together a transitory series of experiences to form a seemingly lasting difficulty. In reality, the elements of their problems are constructed into a unity and taken for granted. Through meditation practice, these fixed perspectives can be unraveled, revealing an opening where something new can emerge.

Meditate on Impermanence

Meditation returns us to moment-by-moment experience, as if we could watch each frame of the movie of our lives and become aware of each flickering picture behind our sense of a constant reality. By following the flow of experience as it unfolds, we can become aware of how our sense of self is created as well.

Exercise 2.1: Applying Impermanence

Contemplate this idea: We have no direct proof, without any doubt, that the object we measure today is identical to the object we measure tomorrow. Time, by a succession of instances, gives us the convincing illusion of continuous existence, and as a result, we create the perceived world with our consciousness.

The objects of our mind appear fixed, permanent, and lasting. But can you look beyond the appearances to the deeper transitory empty nature? Take a particular example, such as the emotion you feel toward someone. Look beyond the various moods you have. Consider how this person is changing, day by day. Look back over past years and ahead to the future. Try to grasp a deeper sense of that person, beyond your opinions and concepts of him or her.

DIFFERENT KINDS OF CHANGE

Certain forms of meditation make it easier to observe that things are undergoing change. Understanding specific kinds of changes can open your clients to a broader understanding of change in general. With a better sense of how change in general happens, clients then can gain tools for making it happen in specific situations.

The ancient Chinese text *I Ching, The Book of Changes* (Wilhelm & Wilhelm, 1995), provides insight about the nature of change itself. The *I Ching* distinguishes three kinds of changes: cyclical, developmental, and immutable law that works through the other transformations.

The first transformation is cyclical: one thing changes into another but eventually is restored back to the original. An example of cyclical change is the seasons, in which summer inevitably becomes fall, then winter, spring, and back to summer again. Many psychological problems take a cyclical form. Sleep and eating disorders, anxiety, and moods are a few examples of problems that may recur in cycles. People can get to know their cycles, which will help them to be better able to predict, attune, respond, and redirect for a more balanced flow.

Exercise 2.2: Contemplate Cyclical Change

Take a few moments to think about your cycles of habits, such as eating and sleeping. Do you have regular habits, such as going to bed at the same time each night and arising at a certain hour each day? Perhaps you see one pattern during the week and another on weekends. Or maybe you do not have any regular pattern for your sleep/wake cycle. Observe your eating habits. Do you have three regular meals each day? Perhaps you snack at a certain time each day or night. Or maybe you have an erratic eating cycle. Now observe your emotional ups and downs. Do you feel positive in the morning and then negative late at night? Or do you observe another daily or even weekly cycle of emotion? Do the cycles correspond with a season or perhaps with patterns from someone you are close to? As you contemplate, don't judge whether the patterns are good or bad; simply observe the timing and rhythm of your cycles. Then you can use your tendencies in the service of the efforts you are making.

A second form of change is progressive development. Transformation takes place a little at a time always moving forward. A life span is a good example of progressive development. People are born, live, grow older and older, and then they die. Change is not just linear. You might not notice the changes that occur day by day, but over a longer period, change becomes easier to detect, such as the obvious transformation from childhood to adulthood. Each stage of development is linked to the former one, like the development of an oak tree from an acorn. Many psychological problems have a progressive development and progressive resolution. Changes may take time.

Exercise 2.3: Contemplate Developmental Change

Now think about the progression of your problem through your life. Can you remember a time before you were bothered by your problem? When did you first notice it? How has it progressed through the years? Have you seen times when it is worse and then better? Make note of your patterns over time.

The third type of change is the immutable law that works through the other transformations. Change begins small, almost unnoticeably. But as things go through their transformations, changes multiply exponentially, with enormous results. For example, clients may not report much change from one session to the next. But many years later, a client who has successfully gone through the therapeutic process often will report many large changes in lifestyle, emotions, and thoughts. The *I Ching* points out that even heaven and earth began small and evolved over eons of time to become the complex universe of today. Figure 2.2 shows the transformations on a universal scale.

Exercise 2.4: Contemplate Change from Small to Large

Imagine that you throw a pebble into a pond. Can you visualize the ripples that spread out from the center to spread through the whole pond? From just one small pebble, the whole pond is filled with ripples. Similarly, making one small change in your own routines can send healing ripples through your whole life. Beginning now, with this quiet moment of contemplation, imagine that the small changes you make as you read through this book and try the exercises can send ripples through your life in positive directions.

CONCLUSION

The discovery that the brain has the ability to change from what we experience presents great hope for our ability to make significant changes, not just

Figure 2.2   Wu Chi Tai Chi

in thoughts and feelings but also in the very structure and function of the brain. We can make our lives and our brains better by what we do. And we can do so at any age. Recognizing that change takes different forms offers different possibilities for interventions. Thus, adding a meditation component to your therapy will elicit positive plasticity in your clients, making it easier for them to regulate their emotions, make sound judgments, and live happier lives.

Part II

Neuroscience

3

The Inner Thread: Effects of All Forms of Meditation

Core Principle 3: Meditation Has a Dual Effect: Calm Alertness

---

Taking your own body and mind as the laboratory, see if you can use these different techniques: that is to say, engage in some thorough-going research on your own mental functioning, and examine the possibility of making some positive changes within yourself.
—The Dalai Lama and H. C. Cutler, The Art of Happiness

INTRODUCTION

Why has meditation become such a widely accepted intervention for modern therapy? The answer has to do with the healing effects of meditation on the mind, brain, and body. Neuroscience research reveals therapeutic qualities that all forms of meditation share in common. This chapter explains the common features shared by all forms of meditation, qualities that can help your clients to enhance their therapeutic process.

ENHANCING RELAXATION IS THERAPEUTIC

Relaxation techniques have been part of psychotherapy since the 1930s, when Edmund Jacobson (1888–1983) introduced progressive relaxation to help people let go of tension and find a deep state of calm.

Jacobson began his research in 1908 at Harvard University, where he uncovered a connection between excessive tension in the muscles and a wide range of physical and psychological disorders. His experiments showed that reducing muscle tonus decreased activations in the nervous system. Thus, relaxation, which involves reducing muscle tonus, brought a lowering of excitation in the central nervous system, which provided a general remedy for many psychological disturbances. By progressively tightening and then loosening the muscles of each part of the body, people could get control of their tensions and let them go. Through the process, they became relaxed overall. Following 20 years of research, Jacobson published his results in *Progressive Relaxation* (1929), where he claimed that research had found his relaxation method had therapeutic effects. His popular book, *You Must Relax* (1934), brought the method to the general population. He wrote that he continued to research his method for 50 years. With so many years of careful research to back him up, Jacobson's progressive relaxation technique became the gold standard for stress relief used in psychotherapy. Research with newer methods had to demonstrate equivalent efficacy by comparison with the progressive relaxation technique.

Researchers have shown that meditation is also an excellent method for calming the nervous system. The practice of meditation activates a relaxation response from the parasympathetic nervous system (the calming part of the nervous system). A meta-study that collected 31 studies together showed that meditation is beneficial for calming down (Dilbeck & Orme-Johnson, 1987). When you perform many of the different forms of meditation, you will find your body and mind become calm and relaxed. Thus, simply taking some time to meditate can enhance the natural ability to be calm.

HOW MEDITATION IMPROVES ON PROGRESSIVE RELAXATION: MEDITATION'S DUAL EFFECT

When meditation was first introduced to the West, people wanted to know how it was better than progressive relaxation. Neuroscience has revealed that meditation not only relaxes, but it also does more.

Neuroimaging technologies reveal that meditation has a dual effect: Certainly, meditation had been shown to bring relaxation. But meditators were able to remain alert and aware at the same time as they relaxed. Neuroscience studies have revealed this interesting dual effect from regular meditation practice, where the nervous system both relaxes and activates simultaneously. Mind and body become relaxed while attention and perception are sharpened. These two opposite changes occur simultaneously and are specifically helpful for therapeutic work. Researchers (Lutz, Gretschar, Rawlings, Ricard, & Davidson, 2004) proposed that the dual effect decouples attention from arousal during meditation. (See Figure 3.1.) This decoupling has many benefits for therapy, because it allows clients to observe and accept their experience with calm attention, even when it might be painful, traumatic, or negative. The regular practice of meditation helps people to face their problems with clear perception and at the same time, inner calm. This ability to be alert and calm simultaneously is extremely helpful for lowering stress, calming anxiety, surmounting trauma, lifting depression, and conquering substance abuse.

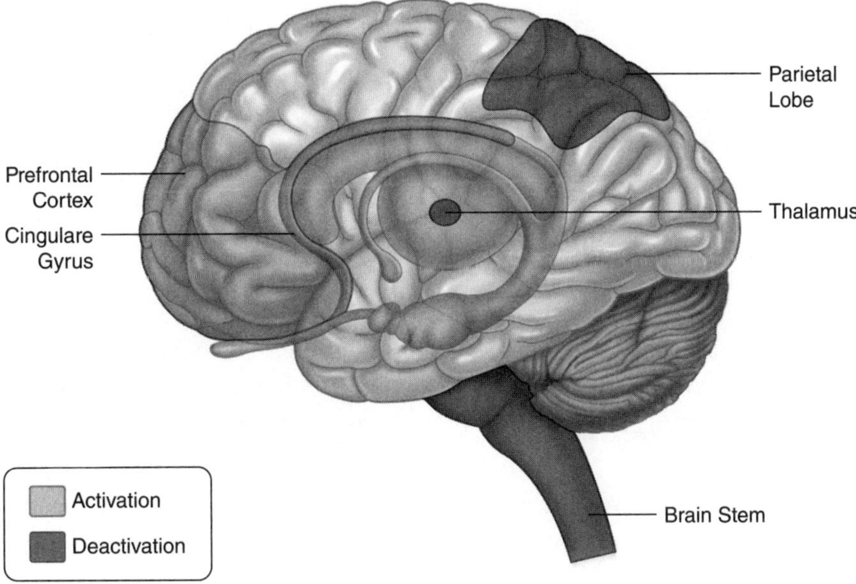

Figure 3.1   Meditating Brain Dual Effect

Electroencephalograph (EEG) studies show that meditators have two different kinds of brainwaves spreading through the activated regions, longer alpha and theta, that correlate with relaxation, and shorter beta and gamma waves, that correspond to alert attention (Hugdahl, 1996). These EEG readings are evidence that not only is the brain more relaxed during meditation, but it is also activated for sharp attention. Bhatia, Kumar, Kumar, Pandey, & Kochupilla (2003) corroborated the earlier findings, showing in their own research that meditators were simultaneously alert and calm with both the longer and shorter EEG brainwave patterns occurring together.

Research by Lutz et al. (2004) also found that this dual effect of corresponding relaxation and alertness is reflected in the brain waves. In the normal waking state, attention and arousal occur together: With focused attention usually comes higher arousal. So, when we pay close attention to something, we typically get tense as the brain is stimulated. Beta waves in the EEG signature reflect this alert attention. You have probably experienced this combination of alertness and tension when working and concentrating. But research has shown that meditators can be highly attentive while remaining deeply relaxed. During meditation, people remain able to be highly alert and aware, yet they tend to have lower heart rates and slower breathing, which are qualities of relaxation. Attention becomes more flexibly able to focus on whatever is needed without being overly tense (Lazar et al., 2005). This may be a result of a wave synchrony, where the brainwaves fire at the same time, unifying the dual effect. During meditation, experienced meditators can bring about synchrony.

MEDITATION INCREASES FEELINGS OF WELL-BEING AND BRAIN COHERENCE

Psychotherapy helps people to resolve problems and overcome difficulties. But it also strives to elicit positive feelings, greater happiness, and an experience that everything is okay. Typically, we refer to these kinds of experiences as *well-being.* Research shows that meditation does indeed bring about feelings of well-being. Even a short practice session can improve how people feel, regardless of how they felt before they started the meditation session (Kohr, 1977).

Studies of many different forms of meditation have found that meditation improves the quality of life. For example, studies of yoga have concluded that meditation can improve functioning in general on a number of measures, including better memory and productivity, reduced anxiety, improvements in hypertension and sleeplessness, as well as converting loneliness into solitude (Dhar, 2002). Mindfulness has also been shown to play a role in psychological well-being. Jon Kabat-Zinn (1992) is a pioneer in research on mindfulness for stress reduction. He has found that mindfulness practice elicits definite feelings of well-being and that mindfulness practice provides many health benefits. B. Alan Wallace, another experienced meditation researcher, believes that building bridges between psychology and some of the meditative practices from Buddhism can help in the quest for mental balance and well-being (Wallace & Shapiro, 2006). These and many other studies offer encouraging evidence about the ability to influence one's level of happiness by engaging in regular meditation.

EEG coherence has been shown to increase between and within the cerebral hemispheres during meditation. EEG coherence is a quantitative index of the degree of long-range spatial ordering of brain waves. Higher coherence means that more of the brain is being used and is associated with improved quality of attention and feelings of well-being. Badawi, Wallace, Orme-Johnson, and Rouzere (1984) found that among meditators with two years of meditation experience, coherence began to spread before meditation sessions. Halfway through the meditation period, coherence spread to both higher and lower frequencies. High coherence continued into the eyes-opened period after meditation. During meditation, even new meditators showed an increase in EEG coherence.

In a comparative study of advanced Tibetan Buddhist and Vedic tradition meditators, Hankey (2006) also found increased brain coherence. Hankey speculated that by activating larger areas of the brain, meditators are moving toward better use of the brain's potential. This activation could lead to enhanced mental development in general.

Another study by Lutz et al. (2004) compared longtime Tibetan Buddhist meditators to people exposed to a short course in meditation. The experienced meditators had a higher gamma wave baseline, synchronized across both hemispheres of the brain (See Figure 3.2). Higher gamma indicates that attentive processes were integrated among many parts of the brain. Gamma is associated with attention and working memory.

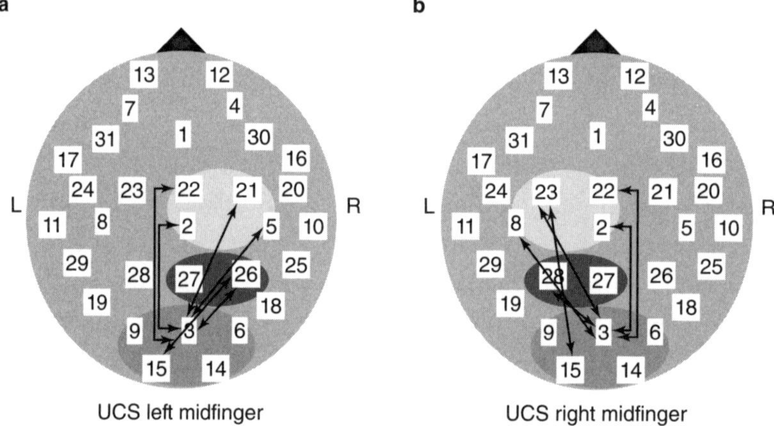

Figure 3.2   Gamma Wave Coherence

MEDITATION ENHANCES AFFECT REGULATION

One of the hallmarks of successful therapy is when clients learn to manage their emotions well; this is known as emotional regulation. Neuroscience research shows that through the process, the brain literally adds more connections between the frontal lobes and the limbic system. In general, certain parts of the limbic system are involved in emotional regulation. The amygdala registers our emotional reactions, telling us how salient, or important, this experience is emotionally. The right amygdala processes negative emotions and the left amygdala processes positive emotions. Many clients have overactivation in the right amygdala. The cingulate gyrus monitors conflict and pain. The anterior insula registers internal body sensations. When people regulate their emotions, there is a deactivation of the right amygdala and more connections between the frontal lobes, cingulate gyrus, anterior insula, and amygdala.

Many studies have shown that meditation enhances the ability to regulate emotions. A recent meditation study by Tang et al. (2009) measured the physiological and brain changes of subjects before, during, and following five days of meditation training. The subjects were compared to a control group who practiced relaxation but not meditation. The meditation group was better able to regulate their emotional reactions than the control group. This helpful effect of meditation on how people handle their emotions correlates with real and lasting changes in the emotional and thinking centers of the brain, including the frontal lobes, insula, amygdala, and cingulate gyrus, all areas that are key to emotional regulation.

Frontal Lobe Improvements

Meditative practices stimulate attentional areas in the frontal lobes, which are key for clear thinking and better decision making. One study found that people who meditated regularly for about 45 minutes a day over a number of years had thicker prefrontal cortices (an area that regulates attentiveness) than nonmeditators who were the same age (Lazar et al., 2005). Developing the prefrontal cortex is key for the ability to think more broadly, reframe, and become more cognitively flexible, which are important therapeutic skills.

Labeling emotions is another part of therapeutic work. Researchers have proposed that affect labeling could be a key component in many mental disorders and that therapy helps by helping clients to better understand their emotions when they can put the experience into words. One study by Creswell, Way, Eisenberger, and Lieberman (2007) showed that mindfulness meditation affected the areas of the brain in the prefrontal cortex that are involved with affect labeling and concluded that this may be how meditation, which radically alters the process of labeling, is helpful.

Insula Increases

The insula is another important part of the brain's emotion system. The insula is located deep within the lateral sulcus that separates the temporal and parietal lobes. It is involved with many basic emotions, such as anger, fear, disgust, happiness, and sadness. It has close interaction with the thalamus, the hallway through which sensory input passes as it is sent on to the cortex for processing. And the insula also shares information with the amygdala, the gateway for recognizing and feeling the emotions. The insula acts as a bridge between the sensory and emotional systems as it receives information from the thalamus and sends output to the amygdala as well as to the prefrontal cortex.

Regular meditation alters the insula in helpful ways. The meditators in one groundbreaking meditation study by Sara Lazar and colleagues (2005) were found to have more thickness than nonmeditators in the anterior (front) part of the insula. Greater thickness in the insula can make it easier to regulate emotions and make better decisions. The anterior part of the insula is involved in awareness of internal body experiences, known as interoception (Craig, 2002, 2009). Lazar saw a correlation between thickness in the anterior insula from meditation and enhanced social feelings of empathy, compassion, fairness, and cooperation.

Increased Gray Matter in Cingulate Gyrus Adds to Emotional Regulation

The cingulate gyrus is located on the inside of the prefrontal cortex and above the corpus callosum, the fibers that connect the two hemispheres. Research has found that increasing the connections between the cingulate gyrus with the frontal lobes, insula, and limbic system leads to better emotional regulation in general (Posner, Rothbart, Sheese, & Tang, 2007). This cingulate area is involved in many aspects of our emotional life, including motivated behavior, spontaneity, and creativity. The cingulate gyrus also processes focus on complex behavior and focus of attention. The cingulate gyrus is primary for the emotional reaction to pain and the regulation of aggressive behavior. It has also been found to play an important role in maternal attachment, as evident in behaviors like nursing (MacLean, 1985). Therefore, increasing the interconnections through the cingulate gyrus has a positive effect on the ability to deal well with emotions.

The Tang, Lu, Geng, Stein, Yang, and Posner (2010) research group found measurable structural changes in the brain following a brief meditation course. They discovered that in the meditating group, the white matter connectivity increased between the anterior (front part) of the cingulate gyrus and other structures of the brain. Thus, meditation seems to literally enhance the neural networks that help regulate emotions.

Britta Hotzel's group (Hotzel et al., 2011) also found structural increases in brain areas involved in emotional regulation following an eight-week mindfulness program. Through pre- and posttesting using anatomical magnetic resonance images of 16 healthy adults, they found increased gray matter in a number of key areas as compared to 17 control subjects placed on a waiting list. They observed increases in the cingulate gyrus, the hippocampus, the temporal-parietal junction, and the cerebellum.

They concluded that these increases reflect superior emotional regulation, improved learning and memory, enhanced self-referential processing, and more flexible perspective taking.

CONCLUSION

The studies discussed in this chapter are a few selections from the many that show how well meditation assists people in improving their ability to regulate their emotions. With research to back you up, you can be confident in adding meditation to your bag of therapeutic techniques.

4

Variations: Different Forms of Meditation

Core Principle 4: There Are Different Forms of Meditation. Pick the Suitable One for Your Client.

Activity and tranquility are one. If it is in accord with the Principle of Nature, the mind that is empty and tranquil at midnight will be the same mind that responds to events and deals with affairs now.
—**W. T. Chan,** *A Sourcebook in Chinese Philosophy*

INTRODUCTION

The word *meditation* tends to conjure up an image of a clear, calm mind, which is true of meditation in general, as we discussed in Chapter 3. But even though different meditation traditions share much in common, meditation is not just one thing or one technique. In reality, there are many different forms of meditation, each with different effects on the mind and brain. Just as you wouldn't use the same therapeutic intervention with every client or problem, you don't have to use the same meditation method with every client and every problem. Through each kind of meditative practice, attention is directed in a particular way. You can choose the best form of meditation to elicit the therapeutic change your client needs. We will guide you in the use of different forms of meditation throughout the book and multimedia that are part of this package. Each type of meditation has a somewhat different effect on how you feel and think. Thus, you can pick and choose, to apply the best form of meditation for your purpose.

The many forms of meditation can be grouped into three general categories: *focus meditations* (Jensen, Kaiser, & Lachaux, 2007; Zhang, Chen, Bressler, & Ding, 2008); *open-focus meditations* (Cahn, Delome, & Polich, 2010); and *no-focus meditations* (Travis & Shear, 2010). Each has different effects, which show up as a distinct EEG pattern. As you come to understand the differences, you will be able to apply the best meditation for each client's problem and situation.

FOCUS MEDITATIONS

There is no limit to the power of the human mind. The more concentrated it is, the more power is brought to bear on one point. That is the secret.
—Vivekananda, The Yogas and Other Works

In this quotation, the great yoga philosopher Vivekananda captured the essence of focus meditation practice and its benefits. Focus meditation involves the concentration of attention. This form of meditation narrows attention down to a single point, away from extraneous distractions. The focal point for attention is held steady without moving. Yoga is a good example of focus meditation. The word *yoga* means to link, yoke, or join together. Yoga practices help people to connect mind, body, and spirit together and to focus on that unity. One of the key benefits is that these practices train people to direct their attention at will and hold it on something chosen.

Some Types of Focus Meditations

There are many different ways to perform focus meditations. For example, withdrawal of the senses (*pratyahara*) is a yoga training that guides in how to narrow the focus of attention and hold it steady. This kind of meditation teaches how to stop thinking about the myriad of things that flow continuously through the mind and to instead narrow attention down to one thing. We all have this capacity built in but aren't skilled with doing it deliberately or sustaining it. For example, if you hear a very loud noise, your attention is automatically withdrawn from whatever you might have been thinking about and directed to the sound. You can develop the capacity to narrow your focus and hold it steady through practice. Many clients who are dealing with disturbing life situations will find this a valuable skill.

The yoga practice of concentration of the mind (*dharana*) is a good example of meditation that keeps attention concentrated on a certain topic or area of concern, in order to delve deeply into it. Thus, the focus of attention is broader than pratyahara, but still held steady. Think of this form of meditation somewhat like a dog on a rope that can wander around as far as the rope permits but no farther. We have all experienced a variation of this meditation when deeply immersed in studying a topic we care deeply about. Often we will study related topics in order to gain broad understanding of the primary concern. Focus meditation trains people to focus attention on their psychological problems and stay focused as they follow a path that is significant to therapy.

Breathing (*pranayama*) meditations are good examples of keeping attention focused on something. These practices keep attention directed to one object of focus while disregarding extraneous things. Neuroscience has shown why focus on breathing is particularly helpful. Breathing meditations activate the vagus nerve, which is the cranial nerve that links the brain with the lungs, heart, and stomach. When performing a simple breathing meditation, we stabilize and calm the mind and body through the nervous system.

Yoga postures (*asanas*) help to make the body an object of focus. Attention is directed to body positioning, which fosters better body awareness, flexibility, and strength. When modified for therapy, these posture practices have therapeutic benefits by helping clients to develop better body awareness and balance. These effects have a bottom-up effect on the mind, bringing calm and emotional regulation.

As you have undoubtedly seen in your clinical practice, when people have emotional problems, they often have difficulty directing and sustaining attention to practical matters. This can make it difficult for them to cope well with their life's tasks and even make it hard to carry out your interventions. You can use these focus meditations to train your clients in skills that will help alleviate some of their suffering and better succeed in therapy and in life.

For example, a college student felt her mind was hijacked by disturbing thoughts whenever she felt stressed. Facing a test or deadline on a homework assignment just made things worse. Focus meditations were a valuable tool to help her gain control of her concentration. She especially liked the experience of mastery, that *she* could do something to help herself when the thoughts swept through her mind. The experience of mastery gave her confidence in the therapy and motivated her to try hard in working through the source of her conflicts. Clients who feel overwhelmed and helpless enjoy mastering a skill that can set a therapeutic process in motion and give better self-control. When attention is focused, outside distractions are minimized. You can imagine how this form of meditation would be helpful for clients who have difficulty concentrating or are bothered by disturbing thoughts or circumstances. These meditations are also helpful when people have to endure discomforts they might not be able to escape or change, as they give people a tool for shifting attention away from being bothered by things out of their control, and toward something more positive that they can do something about.

Brain Areas Involved in Focused Attention

A number of distinct brain areas help coordinate selecting an object and focusing on it. Selective attention activates the temporal-parietal junction, the ventrolateral prefrontal cortex, the frontal eye fields, and the intraparietal sulcus. Sustaining attention involves the right frontal and parietal areas and the thalamus. The thalamus is the gateway to the senses, and researchers have found that a certain area of the thalamus, the lateral geniculate nucleus, helps to direct attention to a relevant area in the visual field (Dantzker, 2006).

Another feature of focused attention, meta-attention, directs attention to the process of attention itself. Meta-attention is also developed during meditation. During focused meditation, the meditator learns to notice when attention drifts away toward something else, which is sometimes thought of as mind wandering. *Attention monitoring* or *conflict monitoring* helps cope with this shifting of attention (Lutz, Brefczynski-Lewis, Johnstone, & Davidson, 2008). Attention monitoring is the process whereby the meditator notices that he or she is not paying attention. When attention is found to be wandering, it is brought back to the object of focus. Unique brain areas become involved: the dorsal anterior cingulate cortex, which is especially activated during error detection and decision making, and the dorsolateral prefrontal cortex, which is activated for the functions of planning, organization, and regulation of thought with action.

Meditators doing focused meditation who were measured with EEG recorded gamma and beta waves. These shorter, quicker brainwaves correlate with deliberately paying attention. Thus, EEGs show that focus meditation activates the attention-regulating centers of the brain. People can learn to direct their thoughts away from disturbing ruminations and toward more positive and hopeful thoughts. Focus meditations, such as focus on breathing, also brings relaxation and calm that activates the calming part of the nervous system, the parasympathetic nervous system, which has a stress-reducing effect.

OPEN-FOCUS MEDITATION

Attention can also have a broad, open focus. Mindfulness is one of the premier examples of open-focus meditation. Mindfulness involves paying attention in the present moment. Attention is free to move to whatever emerges, and so, mindfulness allows attention to move and flow flexibly. Thus, the object of focus changes through time. Compassion meditations are another type of open-focus meditations. When practicing compassion meditations, the focus of attention is on feelings of compassion, but these feelings vary, depending on where and to whom they are directed. Similar to mindfulness, an open-focus form of meditation, in compassion meditation, the object of focus is continually changing and attention is free to move, moment by moment.

For some kind of psychological problems, attention becomes stuck in redundant patterns of thought and emotion. Clients with these problems are out of step with what is actually happening and thus unable to respond realistically to the ongoing situations of life. Mindfulness offers a helpful corrective, giving clients the tools they need to attune to their life as it unfolds. One impulsive, angry client we had said the only way he knew he was angry was when he found himself in the middle of a fight. And he got into fights often. Mindfulness helped him to become aware of his emotions as they were building. We taught him how to practice mindfulness (instructions in Chapter 9). Once he could do it in the office, we encouraged him to try it during the week, to notice what was happening *before* he got into fights. He became aware of things that bothered him—triggers. This awareness gave him choices. He realized that many of his fights were not really necessary. He could work things out or ignore the situation. Mindful awareness taught him to solve problems without having to resort to violence. Mindfulness is also helpful for stress reduction and developing feelings of well-being. Many clients can benefit from this practice to gain deeper self-awareness, learn to relax, and gain good feelings about themselves and others.

Brain Areas Involved in Open Meditation

Focused attention uses a number of specific brain areas, but open meditation engages more of the brain. This kind of open-ended attention was measured using EEGs. Experienced meditators evoke a measurable high-amplitude pattern of gamma synchrony, a dynamic and global reaction across the whole brain (Lutz, Slagter, Dunne, & Davidson, 2008b). These highly synchronized brain states can promote neuroplasticity and enable people to learn new things, especially for more challenging cognitive and emotional functions, because of the integrative and widely distributed neural processes that are involved.

The open-focus form of meditation does not involve any particular attentional focus, and so it does not activate the brain areas that are usually part of attentional focus. Instead, the brain areas involved in monitoring what we experience, staying vigilant, and disengaging our attention from distractions are activated. Open meditation tends to engage processes involved in monitoring ongoing body experiences, such as perception of temperature and pain responses processed by the anterior insula, the somatosensory cortex, and the anterior cingulate cortex.

This form of meditation also reduces the need for voluntary attentional effort or control while remaining focused and concentrated. Psychological tests showed meditators who had expertise in open forms of meditation could detect stimuli quickly with a more economical use of attentional resources than control subjects (Slagter et al., 2007). This has led to characterizing open meditation as a dynamical global state that is activated moment by moment rather than under top-down control, as in focused attention forms of meditation (Lutz et al., 2008b).

When people who were doing open-focus meditation were measured on EEGs, their brains showed an increase in alpha waves. Alpha waves are associated with relaxed attention. Meditation's dual effect shows that people are able to be alert and relaxed at the same time. In addition, mindfulness led to an increase in theta waves in the frontal and temporal-central areas, so crucial for regulating emotions. Theta waves correlate with relaxed attention that monitors inner experiencing, creativity, deeply relaxed tranquility, and restful alertness. It makes sense to find alpha and theta waves correlated with these nondirected forms of meditation that involve monitoring of ongoing experience in a relaxed, flowing, and open way.

NO-FOCUS MEDITATION

In both focus and open-focus meditations, attention is directed to *something*. But a third form of meditation is objectless—directing attention to nothing: the empty moment without thought. This form of meditation is practiced by first noticing any objects that appear in the stream of consciousness and then letting them go. We are accustomed to thinking about things. Our consciousness is filled with thoughts, feelings, and sensations, along with our secondary interpretations and concepts about them. But the ability to meditate on nothing, without turning attention toward an object, can also be developed over time. Thus troubling reflexes can be changed.

No-focus meditation is practiced as part of most major spiritual traditions, such as yoga, Zen, Taoism, Tibetan Buddhism, and Transcendental Meditation. For example, in yoga, no-focus meditation is known as the stage of deep meditation (*dhyana*), characterized by the absence of both focus and effort. In this state, practitioners develop a clear consciousness, centered in the present moment, free of obstructions from intruding thoughts. Then they can simply respond automatically and effortlessly.

Clients who suffer from depression, bipolar disorder, trauma, or anxiety can find great relief from no-focus meditations. These practices turn the meditator away from redundant rumination on problems, thereby sending a ripple of calm through the entire nervous system and leading to a lowering of stress and a natural return to healthy balance. In our practice, we taught this technique to an elderly client who was depressed about being old, even though she had the potential for many positive years ahead. She spent much of her time ruminating and complaining, barely noticing the love, caring, and concern her family extended to her. She benefited from being able to clear away disturbance. Then, with a momentary relief from despair, she became open to the present moment. She saw the smile on her little grandson's face and felt the warm embrace from her daughter. This skill of no-focus meditation can help people become aware of the positive potentials they often miss.

Brain Areas Involved in No-Focus Meditation

No-focus meditation such as in Zen meditation, where meditators are thinking about nothing, being unfocused and undifferentiated, is not processed top down or mediated by deliberate, higher-level cortical activity. Instead, the brain goes through a series of more generalized brain states, where each state becomes the source for the next one, integrating together for regulating the meditative experience. Pagnoni, Cekic, and Guo (2008) found that the default mode network is activated during Zen practice. The default mode network is linked to the automatic stream of thoughts that occurs when we aren't goal-directed or thinking about anything in particular. Zen meditation is a practice that develops heightened awareness while clearing the mind of conceptual content. Using functional magnetic resonance imaging (fMRI), these researchers determined that Zen meditators showed a better ability to regulate the automatic flow of associations.

The EEG associated with no-focus meditation was shown to correlate with a very intense type of alpha wave (Travis & Shear, 2010). These alpha waves tend to occur when people have relaxed attention while remaining alert without really trying to do so. And these waves accompany experiences of well-being and comfort.

CONCLUSION

All three forms of meditation have healing benefits. Each method gives you a unique ability to work with the flow of consciousness under every circumstance, an invaluable skill both for bringing therapeutic change in your clients and for your own life.

Part III
Tools of Meditation

5

Attention

Core Principle 5: Train Attention to Enhance Meditation and Improve Therapy Outcomes.

Everyone knows what attention is. It is the taking possession by the mind, in clear and vivid form, of one out of what seem several simultaneously possible objects or trains of thought. Focalization, concentration of consciousness, are of its essence.

—William James, The Principles of Psychology

What Do You See?

A meditation master had been hired by a high school to help the basketball team improve their free throws. As the team lined up, the master proposed a competition in which the person with the best answer would take the shot. He called for the first contestant. One team member, a well-liked crowd-pleaser, stepped up to the line and faced the basket. The master asked him, "What did you see?"

(continued)

(*continued*)

The player answered confidently and quickly, "I see the walls and bleachers, the spectators, the floor, the net, and my girlfriend sitting over there—hi, Jenny!" The whole team shouted an enthusiastic cheer. He shot, missing completely, as the ball sailed into the stands. The master frowned and shook his head. The player laughed and sat down next to his teammates who offered a consoling pat on the back. The master called another team member to the line.

The master asked him, "What do you see?"

The player answered, "I see the backboard and the net." His shot hit the backboard and bounced off the ring into the net.

The master showed a glimmer of approval as he motioned for the player to return to his seat. Then he turned to the star shooter, calling him to the line. The shooter stepped up, paused, took a breath, and looked straight ahead at the basket. The master asked him, "What do you see?"

The shooter spoke clearly and with conviction, "I see the path: the ball to the goal of the hoop: an opening, empty space."

When the master handed the shooter the ball, he bounced it a few times and then threw. The ball sailed in a graceful arc directly through the hoop without even touching the rim. The master just smiled.

INTRODUCTION

The star shooter in "What Do You See?" understands the value of paying attention when he shot, which played a central role in his success. William James (1842–1910), a founding father of psychology, argued against the prevailing view of his time that attention is simply given. He firmly believed that our experience is largely what we agree to attend to (James, 1896). Thus, when attention is directed correctly, great achievement is possible. Meditation involves attention, and so training it can enhance your skills.

But we rarely give attention much thought. Even when people are practicing a sport such as basketball, they put most of their effort into the physical aspects of shooting. They usually don't consider how they are using their attention. And yet attention is a fundamental element. Correct use of attention can make a difference in many of the things you do. When you use attention correctly, you will do things better, including therapy.

Attention can be trained. Meditative practices have time-honored methods for developing and strengthening attentional capacities. Attention is trained in different ways in meditation, and each of these ways has unique applications for achieving skills. This chapter describes ways of training attention that will prove helpful for learning to meditate. You can teach clients how to direct attention at will and how to deliberately hold it on something. Clients also can practice freeing attention to flow naturally. As their attention abilities improve, your clients will find the different kinds of meditation in Part IV of the volume easier to perform. In addition, skills with attention have many applications that enhance psychological well-being and cognitive function. Attention training can facilitate psychological change, helping to direct it to thoughts, feelings, and behaviors. The details of experiencing may be difficult to pin down, especially when there is suffering. This can make therapeutic intervention more difficult. But when you train attention through meditation, your clients gain more access to what is actually there. Then they will be able to harness their potential for more reality-based reactions.

ABILITY OF ATTENTION

Everyone has an innate ability to pay attention. If we ask you to look up at the ceiling now and pay attention to what you see, you can do so easily. You can sustain your attention by continuing to look at the ceiling if you want to. You can also shift your attention easily—if, for example, we ask you now to pay attention to the wall. These skills of directing attention, sustaining it, and shifting it to something else are built into your mind-brain-body system. In fact, the brain has a highly developed system that engages much of your nervous system in the process. This attentional system is highly integrated with your visual system for looking and with your motor system for moving your eyes and turning your head and body toward what you are attending to. You don't have to think about how to do so, for the system to work. You just do it. But there are ways to make your attentional system work better.

A MODEL FOR HOW ATTENTION WORKS

The unified system of attention involves multiple behavioral states and brain states with a number of subsets of cortical structures (Zillmer, Spires, & Culbertson, 2008, p. 241). The sequence of mental processing during attention takes place in five distinct steps: (1) activate, (2) select, (3) orient, (4) maintain, and (5) act.

The attentional system *activates* from either an external or an internal stimulus. Outer and inner become linked. When you respond to something in the environment that concerns you, and especially when something concerns you internally, you resolve it within the environment. Once you *select* something to focus on, other things are ignored. This is because conscious attentional capacities are limited. You consciously attend to only a few items at once (classically, seven plus or minus two items), so you tend not to notice anything more. This is also referred to as concentration of attention.

Attention tends to *orient* selectively to the most salient, relevant things. This orienting might happen spontaneously, as when your attention is drawn to a thunderclap during a storm. Or attention can be focused deliberately when concentrating, for example, when you turn your attention to reading this chapter. Once oriented to something, attention will *maintain* focus there, until the process is complete. Then you can *act* toward the object of attention.

Generally, the different components of attention involve a combination of top-down (conscious and deliberate) and bottom-up (unconscious and automatic) brain processes. Some parts of attention are deliberate and conscious while other aspects occur automatically, reflexively, without our quite noticing. Top-down attentional capacities are available to your conscious thinking, so they can be accessed intentionally, but, as mentioned, conscious attention is limited. Bottom-up attentional capacities are larger. You attend to far more information unconsciously, even though you may not know it consciously. Meditation develops bottom-up and top-down attention, both of which have helpful applications for therapeutic change, learning, and achieving.

BRAIN AREAS INVOLVED IN ATTENTION

Much of the nervous system gets involved when you pay attention. If something attracts your attention, the reticular formation of the brain stem produces arousal and orients you to it. The autonomic nervous system and endocrine system are both activated as well, bringing about an increase in heart rate and blood pressure. Furthermore, the neurotransmitters dopamine, serotonin, acetylcholine, and norepinephrine are stimulated when you are alerted (Moruzzi & Magon, 1959). This nervous system activation helps you to respond quickly and directly to a stimulus. Your attention automatically responds bottom up to the properties of the stimulus, such as a bright light or a loud sound. And your parietal lobe activates as you focus on the specific relevant location, somewhere in space. So you disengage your attention from stimuli that your attentional system regards as unimportant and direct it to something that the system regards as more relevant. Thus, you activate the top-down system of attention. If the stimulus is something you look at, your visual orienting is activated through the visual pathway. Your eyes saccade, which means they move all around, tracing the object. This eye movement creates a spatial map, which is projected onto your visual cortex. If the stimulus enters through a different sensory input, such as a sound, your auditory cortex registers the stimulus through your ears. A tactile stimulus takes effect through your sense of touch and is processed by the parietal lobes. No matter how the stimulus is perceived, your attentional system responds quickly and automatically, outside of conscious awareness, as a bottom-up process. Therapeutic methods can work with these bottom-up processes, and many of the exercises in this book guide you in using these automatic responses to help your clients.

Once your attention is activated bottom up, it can be concentrated and sustained by combining with top-down processing. Stability, flexibility, and consistency in attentional efforts come from the rostral midbrain structures and the brain stem. The motor cortex and basal ganglia help to keep your attention alerted, connected, and focused to where it was drawn. If you choose to maintain attention there, the executive functions in your frontal and parietal lobes are activated. If you want to shift your attention to something else, the front part of the frontal lobes, the prefrontal cortex, is activated for deliberately redirecting attention. The hippocampus and amygdala also become engaged in the process of encoding into working memory what you are focused on. Thus, it is clear that attention uses much of the brain, functioning both consciously and unconsciously.

ATTENTION TRAINING

You can train the different steps of mental processing in attention: activate, select, orient, maintain, and act. The next series of exercises are designed to make attention more responsive, accurate, stable, and flexible. These skills help clients who are suffering with emotional problems to harness their attention, which may be compromised from dealing with disturbance. These simple exercises have a broader effect as well. They tend to initiate a process of change, offering experiences of mastery and a sense of developing self-control and support.

Attention Training Exercises

A response to a stimulus activates attention, which engages selection and helps you to orient. Then you can process matters, indicating what is important, and take action. But sometimes, especially when people are preoccupied with inner conflicts, attention does not function as it should. Working on resolving disturbances is part of the process, but activating attention toward positive stimuli can have a ripple effect, gently guiding thoughts and feelings away from inner turmoil and toward realistic contact in the present moment. You can train clients to respond and notice with these exercises. Then the appropriate action to take becomes clear to the clients.

Exercise 5.1: Begin with Observation

Observation is an important component for engaging attention. Attend to what you see or sense. The experience will lead to development of attention skills in general.

One natural way to train attention can be drawn from everyday life. Attention is activated by what is around us in everyday life. You can sharpen your activated attention by doing it deliberately in a place with many objects with intense colors, shapes, smells, and variety—the grocery store.

Visit your local grocery store, but don't go to make any purchases. Instead, walk around simply to observe as your attention is activated. Disregard brands, labels, or even what the things are. Instead, notice the colors and patterns and the shapes of the containers without thinking about them. Note how the bright colors, interesting lettering, and packaging shapes draw your attention and how your emotions and impulses are stimulated.

We don't simply observe with our eyes. We can call upon all the senses to enhance observation. Notice how your sense of smell is also activated. Each aisle has characteristic odors. Pay attention to the aromas in the fruits and vegetable aisle. Close your eyes for a moment and observe the odors. Can you identify the food right there? Open your eyes and check. Move around to a few different produce areas and try to identify what it is from the sense of smell. Then move from the produce aisle to the cleaning products section. How do the different aromas affect you? There is a close connection between sensory experiences and the emotions.

Do this observation experiment with your sense of touch. Notice the temperature, texture, and shape of the fruit or vegetable. Can you identify it from simply touching it?

Finally, listen to the sounds that you hear. You might notice people talking, the clanging of carts, or perhaps music playing in the background. Listen carefully as you walk through the store. Do the sounds alter in different sections? All of these inputs activate your attention. When you are aware of the activation, you train your attention to be better attuned to your environment.

Exercise 5.2: Test Your Skills

Walk into a room in your house pause briefly for one minute, then leave. Now attempt to describe everything in the room: the objects, the room itself, the atmosphere, the lighting. If you are doing this alone, you may find it helpful to jot down on paper what you remember. Return and compare the actual experience to your remembered one. Again, now, observe carefully. Spend a bit more time: five minutes. Observe carefully. Then leave and describe the room and its contents. Return. How many things do you notice this time? How detailed is your description?

There are many possible variations of this exercise. Are you more intrigued by auditory experience? If so, try this exercise with an auditory impression. Record a few minutes of sound from somewhere that has a variety of sounds available. Try to recall all that you heard. Replay your recording and compare your experience. You can also perform this exercise using prerecorded music. Try listening to a CD or album that you like, paying careful attention to the details of the rhythm, the bass, the beat, the harmony, the melody, the theme, and so on. Then pause the recording and recall as clearly as possible what you heard. Once again, listen to the actual music and compare it to your memory image.

PRACTICE ATTENTION SKILLS WITH A MANDALA

Exercise 5.3: Activate Attention

Begin by looking at Figure 5.1, which depicts a famous mandala known as the sacred instrument (Sri Yantra). Feel free to pick another object, picture, or piece of art that is interesting to you, if you prefer. Place it in clear view. Sit upright cross-legged on the floor, on a small pillow, or on a straight-backed chair, and

Figure 5.1   Sri Yantra

look at the object. Let your attention be activated toward this picture. Be curious about it, perhaps thinking about all the different shapes, how they are arranged, or perhaps contemplating the symmetry you might observe. Notice as many aspects of the picture that you can see, such as the shapes, patterns, sizes, and even their meaning to you.

Exercise 5.4: Selection Training

Attention can be trained to remain steadily directed to one thing while ignoring other things. Select one part of the Sri Yantra to look at. Are you drawn to the dot in the center? Or perhaps you find patterns toward the outside more interesting. Select one section to look at while ignoring the other parts. Then experiment with selecting another area to look at. Play with making certain selections while ignoring others.

Exercise 5.5: Orienting Training

Now orient to the Sri Yantra. You have looked at it and activated your attentional focus toward this fascinating diagram. The words Sri Yantra mean "sacred instrument." Many different meanings have been attributed to this famous mandala. Traditionally, the intersection of nine triangles that intertwine with each other to produce 43 smaller triangles is thought to represent the entire universe. The center point, known as the bindu, is a symbol for the origin, out of which everything else emerges. And the petals all around are thought to be the lotus of creation. What do you think about these meanings? Do you see others? Let yourself orient toward this symbol to see what you discover in relationship to this mandala.

Exercise 5.6: Maintain Attention Training

Deliberately maintaining attention will train the ability to be steadily involved in something. This can become a great resource for meditation, for psychotherapy, and more generally for accomplishing the tasks of life.

Now keep your attention focused on the mandala only. If your attention wanders away, where does it go? If possible, retrace the links back to the mandala. Otherwise, gently bring your attention back to the object originally selected, noticing the process of doing so. Begin with just two or three minutes of focusing. Gradually increase the time as you become able to maintain focus longer. Skill in maintaining a stable attention improve with practice.

After directing your attention to the Sri Yantra with your eyes open, close your eyes and picture it within. People who are naturally able to form visual pictures will see a vivid image of the picture. For others, the picture may be vague. Keep your attention focused on the image even if it is vague. Notice all the details that you saw when looking at the object, such as the patterns and shapes.

If you find that you have forgotten some of the details, open your eyes to look again. Notice more about it, then close your eyes again and visualize the picture as an inner image. Keep switching between eyes opened to look and eyes closed to visualize for several minutes until you feel that you are able to hold a clear sense of the picture within.

Exercise 5.7: Taking Action

Can you do something with the Sri Yantra? Perhaps you would like to try drawing your own version. Or maybe you would prefer to close your eyes and visualize variations in your imagination. Perhaps you would like to write something about the meanings it has inspired for you. The idea is to do something with this image now. Can you imagine meaningful ratios from the patterns? Can you see parallels to your life's patterns? Does the mandala offer any insights about possible actions in the real world? Notice the interplay of interactions, of patterns in ratios between triangles, symbolic of how this is possible.

DEVELOPING FLEXIBLE ATTENTION

Exercise 5.8: Narrowing in on Something

You can cultivate flexible, responsive attention by deliberately shifting your range of attention. This exercise, drawn from the great yoga tradition of pratyahara, teaches how to shift attention from a broad outer focus to a narrow, inward focus.

Sit comfortably and quietly for a few moments. Then notice what is around you: any aromas, the temperature of the air, the sounds around you, and the quality of the light in the room where you are sitting. Focus on everything surrounding you for several minutes.

Next, turn your attention to whatever is close to you, such as the feeling of your clothing, smooth or textured, loose or tight. Notice the chair you are sitting on, whether it feels hard or soft, warm or cool. How do your feet meet the floor? Are they resting lightly on the floor or pushing against it? Keep your attention focused on what is close to you for several minutes.

Now notice inner body sensations. Scan through your body to notice your muscles. Are you holding them tight, or are your muscles relaxed? Is there any unnecessary tightening? If possible, relax any tensions that can be relaxed. Turn your attention to your breathing. Allow it to be natural as you notice how the breath goes in through your nose and then out again. Perhaps you can sense your pulse or heartbeat.

Finally, withdraw attention from your body sensations to focus on your thoughts. Notice the thoughts as if you are sitting on the bank of a river, watching each thought float by. If your attention wanders back to inner sensations, to other stimuli close to you, or to something else in the outer environment, gently bring attention back to your thoughts as soon as you can. Maintain the focus for several minutes. The ability to withdraw your attention from distractions responds to practice, so repeat this exercise in different rooms of the house or even outdoors.

Exercise 5.9: One-Pointed Attention

The ability to direct attention to a single point and keep it there can be trained. Directing attention in this way is a valuable skill for therapy when you need to become aware of inner concerns and experiences, even if they are uncomfortable. It can also help when learning something new. This exercise introduces this useful one-pointed attention skill. We often present this meditation to children who like to think of their favorite color. In fact, most people have a preference for certain colors, or even one color, which makes it easier to keep attention focused there.

Pick your favorite color. Once you have chosen, close your eyes and think about the color. You might find it easier to see the color fill your perceptual field, the screen of your mind, or you might prefer to think of something specific, an object of that color, such as a blue box, a large green chalkboard, or an enormous yellow sun. Keep your attention directed to the color and only that color. If another thought or other object of interest emerges, gently let it go and return to focusing on the color. With young children or for those with a short attention span, begin with as few as 30 seconds, and gradually increase the time to between two and five minutes. This skill improves dramatically with practice. You will enjoy the experience of control and calm that results.

Exercise 5.10: Flexible Attention

Attention can be narrowly directed to one thing, but it can also be flexible, open, and resilient. People who suffer from psychological problems often are stuck in redundant patterns of thoughts and emotions with attention narrowed down into habitual patterns. Training in flexible attention can begin a change process. The exercise that follows can help to develop a more open, flowing, and flexible use of attention.

Think of your favorite color for a minute or two, as in the previous exercise. Once you have pictured the color for several minutes, imagine that it becomes smaller and smaller, until it shrinks down to a single concentrated dot. Then let it become larger and larger again. For a variation, let the shape change from a square to a circle or to a triangle. You might enjoy allowing the color to change into another color or even become a rainbow of colors. Be playful with the shifting. You can have fun with this exercise, allowing your imagination to alter the image in many creative ways.

CONCLUSION

Attention is a key component of meditation. By training your attention, you develop skills you will use when you meditate. These skills will also prove helpful during psychotherapy, a time when attention is often turned inward to explore and grow. Practice the exercises in this chapter often. Begin with just a few minutes devoted to each exercise, and increase the time as you feel more able to sustain attention. With practice, you will find that your ability to work as you choose with attention becomes part of everyday life, leading to easier mastery of many endeavors.

6

Sensory Awareness

Core Principle 6: Attune Your Senses to Enhance
Self-Awareness.

---

*Your vision will become clear only when you look into your heart.
Who looks outside, dreams. Who looks inside, awakens.*

—Carl Jung

INTRODUCTION

Your senses are your gateway to the world. By turning your attention inward, known in neuroscience as *interoception,* you awaken not only to inner experience but also to the outer world. Sensory awareness provides accurate and attuned information, bringing you in touch with your life as you live it. And by attuning to sensing, both inner and outer, you will enhance one of your key tools to meditation.

The important role of sensing is reflected in the sensory receptors found all through your nervous system, ready to send signals to the brain for processing. Developing your awareness of sensing from touch, vision, sound, taste, and smell develops your embodied awareness of being in the world.

This chapter teaches how to become aware of sensing and follow it. Small experiences can bring you to your senses, starting a gentle process of self-awareness. The practice is simple and concrete, making it easy for most people to do. These skills not only help with meditation but also facilitate the therapeutic process. By taking these first steps, you move closer to noticing deeper feelings, thoughts, and behaviors. Then you can enter the path of awareness.

The Woman Who Learned to Perceive

A young woman came for therapy to treat her depression. Her dark hair nearly covered her eyes, which she directed toward the floor as she spoke in a monotone. She complained about feeling disappointed about her life. All the significant people had let her down, and she resented them for it. She had no real interests. She struggled just to get by, day to day. Life was dull, bleak, and hopeless. We listened quietly, extending warm understanding. Then we offered, "Let's take a walk outside together."

It was a beautiful day, with the sun casting a shimmering glow on the bay near our office. But the client walked with her head down and a frown on her face. As we stepped onto the sand, we said, "Do you see the water?"

"Of course," said the client with a sarcastic note in her voice, lifting her gaze just long enough to glance at the water.

"Can you smell the salt air?" we asked, taking a long breath in.

"Sort of," said the client, making an effort to smell the air. "Yeah, it's salty out there."

"And do you feel the breeze on your face?" we inquired.

We caught a slight flicker of enjoyment in her expression, as the client seemed to register the soft warmth from the gentle wind. "Well, yes," she said with a bit of surprise in her voice.

We walked along. "Do you hear the water lap along the shore?"

The client stopped for a moment to listen to the subtle sound of the water as it flowed over the sand with the rising tide. "Sort of," she said with surprise in her voice.

"And can you feel the sand beneath your feet?" The client moved her foot around as she allowed herself to experience the soft texture. She made a figure-eight pattern with her open-toed sandal, engrossed for a moment in her experiencing.

Then we said softly, "Can you hear the bird calling?"

The client looked up, surprised. Then she smiled broadly as she took a deep breath. "Yes, yes! I didn't notice it before, but now I hear it clearly. How beautiful!"

We made our way back to the office together, silently enjoying the many sensory experiences along the way. By the time we were seated, the client seemed noticeably different. Attuned to her sensing, immersed in the flowing waters of her awareness, she was now more open and eager to engage in the therapeutic process.

THE SENSORY NERVOUS SYSTEM: TOUCH, SOUND, VISION, TASTE, AND SMELL

Many parts of the nervous system are devoted to monitoring sensory experience. Sensing begins with sensory receptor neurons receiving information from the world, such as the eyes for seeing, the skin for touch, the ears for hearing, the nose for smelling, and the mouth for tasting. These afferent neurons conduct impulses inwards to the brain. They are located in the periphery of the body and send signals to neurons located deeper within the nervous system, on the spinal cord and brain. So, for example, you detect a cool sensation from holding a cold glass of water through sensory receptors in your fingers, which convey signals to your central nervous system. There are different types of afferent neurons, each with its own receptor field, to detect different qualities of sensing, such as texture and temperature, helping you to sense a glass you hold in your hand. The spinal cord receives the signals and sends them along ascending pathways from the body to the brain. The signals pass through the lower brain area in the brain stem and up to the thalamus. The word *thalamus* means "hallway" in Greek. And sensory information passes through the thalamus, like traveling through a hall, to be sent on to the specific area of cortex that handles the type of signal sent (see Figure 6.1).

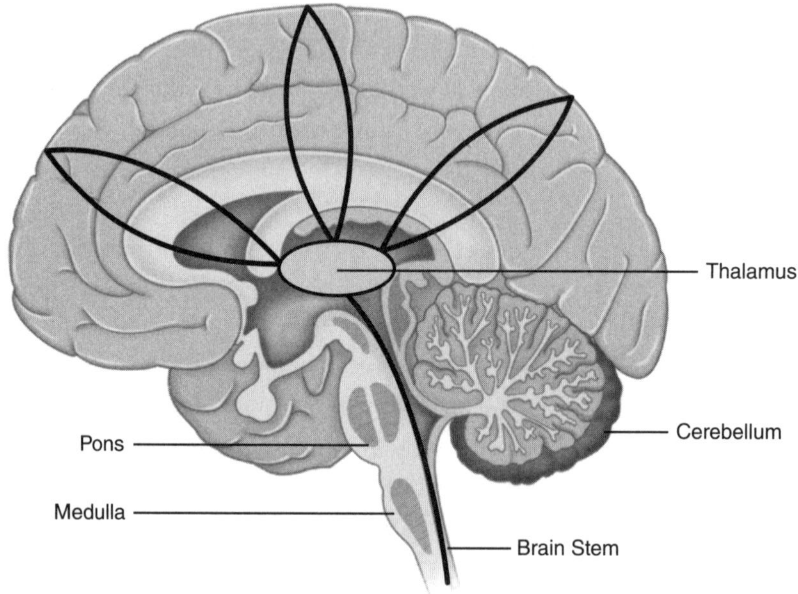

Figure 6.1 Thalamus-Cortical System

Interoception Processing in the Insula

There is research evidence that a key area for our internal body sensing is the insula of the brain (Craig, 2009). The insula is tucked deep within the cortex, in the fissure that divides the frontal, parietal, and temporal lobes. This location makes the insula well placed for integrating information about internal bodily sensations with higher-order emotional processing. The anterior insula contains interoceptive representations (maps) of internal sensory experiencing. These sensory maps in the anterior insula interact closely with the limbic system, providing self-awareness of nuances of body experience during emotion—for example, in anger, sadness, fear, disgust, happiness, and love. Thus, we know what we feel in part because of the associated bodily experiences, as the James-Lange theory of emotion proposed many years previously (Lang, 1994). The modern neuroscience way to express this idea is that our thoughts and feeling are embodied—we are embodied beings. Meditation has been shown to thicken this area of the insula. A thick insula processes more efficiently. This helps to explain why meditation is so helpful for emotional regulation (Lazar, 2005).

Higher-Order Sensory Processing

Higher-order processing of sensory signals from the thalamus and insula takes place on different parts of the cortex. The sense of touch is regulated by the anterior strip of the parietal lobes, which are involved in sensation, body image, and body orientation in space. This sensory strip has a sensory map that corresponds to parts of the body that are used more frequently. So, more area on the cortex is devoted to the hands and face, which we use most often, whereas less area on the cortex is dedicated to the back, for example. This sensory strip interacts with another strip, the motor strip located right in front of the sensory strip, known as the primary motor cortex (Figure 6.2). The Homunculus (Little Man), in Figure 6.3 first drawn by Walter Penfield (1891–1976) following his experiments with epileptic patients undergoing surgery, shows the relative allocation of cortex to different body areas in terms of movement. Similar to the sensory strip, more cortex is devoted to areas we move often, such as the face and hands, whereas less cortex is allocated for the back. These two side-by-side sensory

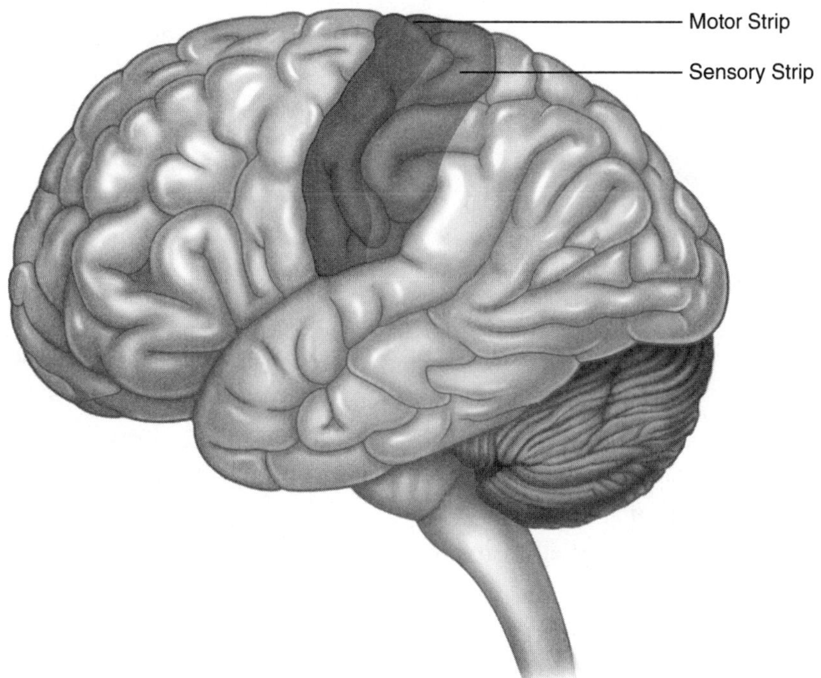

Figure 6.2 Sensory-Motor Cortex

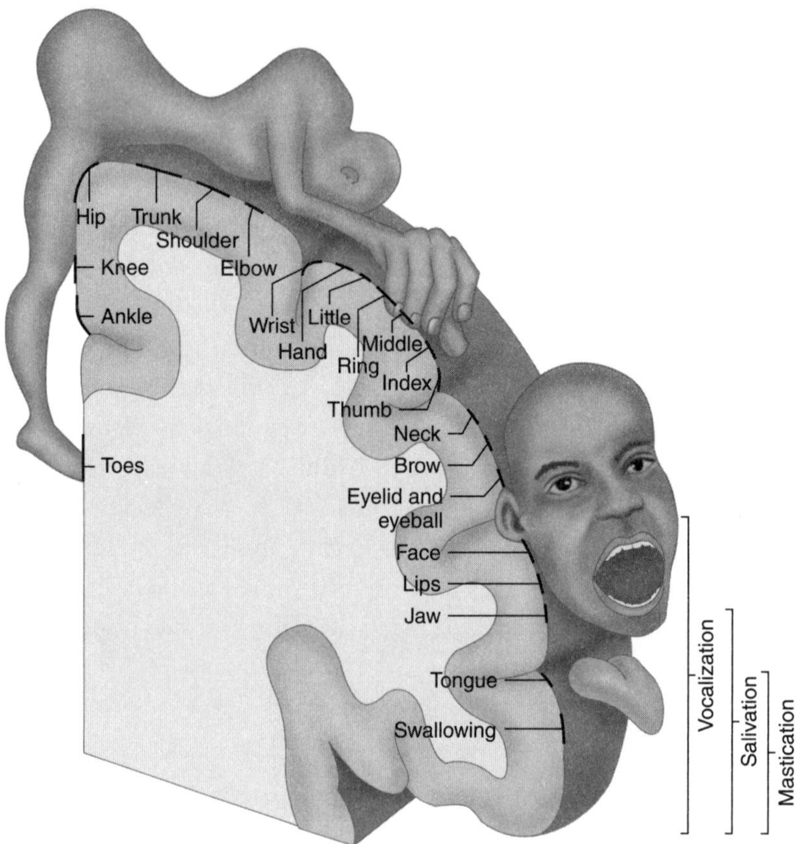

Figure 6.3   Homunculus

and motor strips interact with each other whenever you move, giving you sensory experiences accompanying movement.

Seeing is regulated through the visual cortex in the occipital lobes located in the back of the brain. Hearing is processed in the auditory cortex located close to the ears in the temporal lobes. Smell is regulated by another part of the temporal lobes, and taste is regulated through the gustatory cortex located in the insula.

With so many areas all through the body and nervous system involved in sensory perception, sensing is a vital component of experiencing. Thus, learning to become more attuned through the practice of sensory awareness will enhance functioning in many important ways and on many different levels.

Noticing Your Relationship to the World through Sensory Awareness

Our sensory system has the capacity to attune us accurately to the world. In fact, we are always in relationship to the environment. Many clients are out of touch with their sensory awareness, which interferes with realistic responses to the world. You can help clients to sharpen their senses for better attunement leading to clearer perception and more realistic behavior. These exercises enhance sensory awareness, to help your clients become more grounded in their here and now sensory experience.

ENHANCE YOUR SENSORY AWARENESS OF TOUCH

Begin with one of the senses used often: the sense of touch. Encourage practice of each exercise several times at different points through the day or evening between sessions. As skills build, sensory awareness is enhanced.

Exercise 6.1: Begin with Tapping

You can enhance your sense of touch with simple tapping.

Lightly tap your arm, starting at the shoulder and moving down toward your hand. Make your right wrist loose and tap lightly with your fingers along your left arm. Tap the top, bottom, and sides, covering the entire surface. After several minutes of tapping, stop, close your eyes, and notice the sensations. Next, tap your right arm with the left hand and then take a moment to experience the sensations.

You can use both hands simultaneously to tap your legs, stomach, chest, neck, and back. Take time to notice the sensations after your tapping. You will feel more sensations in the areas following tapping.

Exercise 6.2: Sensing an Object

Clients who have difficulty focusing attention in general may find it easier if you touch an object. In this exercise, experiment with focusing attention on the sense of touch, using a small stone that you find outside. We keep a group of small, smooth stones in our office. You may want to collect some for your office or you could use any small object such as a pen, cell phone, wallet, or watch. This exercise can help to enhance body awareness and the ability to notice sensations in general.

Pick a small stone that interests you. It can be rough or smooth, brightly colored or dull, anything you find visually interesting. Choose one that is a few inches in diameter so that it has a little bit of weight to it. You can also do this exercise with any everyday object, such as a cell phone, pen, or wallet.

Hold one hand out in front of you, palm facing up, and place the stone in the palm of your hand. Focus all your attention on any sensations you feel with the stone on your hand. Can you sense the stone's weight? Is it warmer or cooler than your skin? Can you feel the texture of the stone? Keep your attention focused on the sensations.

Next, remove the stone from your palm, but keep your hand extended as you notice the sensations in your palm. How do these sensations compare with how you felt when the stone was there? Notice the temperature, the air on your skin, or anything else that you perceive.

Now place the stone back in your palm and experience it there once again, paying attention to all the sensations.

Hold your other hand up in front of you, palm up, and compare your two hands. You will notice interesting differences. And finally, remove the stone from your hand and pay attention to both palms. You probably will find it easier to notice your sensations now that you have done these exercises.

For a variation, lie down on your back and place the stone on your stomach. Close your eyes and pay attention to the sensations from the stone resting there. Next, move the stone to different locations on your body, such as your arm or leg, and repeat the exercise. Then take the stone away and pay attention to those areas, noticing the difference. You will find that you have greater body awareness in response to the stone. These exercises are examples of using your senses to have an experience of sensing, just for sensing, not for anything else.

Exercise 6.3: Sensing Temperature

This exercise can sensitize you to your sensory relationship of your body temperature in the environment.

Begin by closing your eyes, and make note of the temperature in your palm by touching the palm of your right hand to your upper left arm. If you are wearing long sleeves, roll up your sleeves so that your palm touches your skin directly.

Take a moment to notice how warm or cool your palm feels in comparison to your arm.

Next, touch a table or chair. How does your palm's temperature feel now? Is it warmer or cooler than before? Give yourself a minute or two to sense the temperature. Now place your palm on your clothes at your shoulder, paying close attention to the temperature of your palm as you do so. Then touch a cool glass of water or perhaps the inside of a refrigerator. Note the temperature of your palm as you are placing it on a cool object. Finally, hold your hand out, palm up, and feel the temperature without touching anything. You can notice how your sensation of temperature is closely related to the context. Try to experience the temperature as it is, not just the temperature you feel when touching an object. Your hand touching an object can be the occasion for the experience of warmth or of coolness, you might say. A Zen master might ask: Where is temperature? Is it in your hand, is it in the object, is it by comparison that you decide it, or is it somewhere else? Where does coolness go when an object becomes warm? Is it relative or is it transitory, like the river in the famous aphorism of Heraclitus, that you never step into twice. The waters ever flow.

Now repeat this experiment, but turn your attention to the textures. So, as you touch your skin, notice the surface as you touch it. You will feel a distinct difference between the texture of your skin, your clothing, a cool glass, or simply holding your palm up in the air.

SENSE OF VISION: WORKING WITH THE TOOLS OF SEEING

Seeing is an important component of sensory experiencing, and, in fact, human beings are highly visual. We rely heavily on our sense of sight, often more than the other senses. You probably have experienced how your vision overrides your other senses when sitting in a gas station. If you observe the car next to you pull away, you may feel as if you are moving backward and quickly press the brake, even though your car didn't move at all.

Although you see through your eyes, you actually see with your brain. Your eyes are your visual sensors. Some preliminary processing of what you see takes place right on the retina of your eyes. However, much of visual processing occurs in your brain. The occipital lobes of the cortex have more than 32 zones for processing the rich varieties of visual experiencing, such as texture, color, and shape. In fact, the visual cortex is sometimes called the striate cortex because all these zones give it a striped appearance. Having such a highly developed visual system, you rely heavily on seeing for orienting to the world.

But how often do you take time to really look? Sometimes you may be seeing without noticing. For example, while you are looking at something, you might be thinking about something else. Or perhaps you are noticing one thing but missing another. The exercises in this section develop your visual sensing, beginning with relaxing your eyes to help you see better and more fully.

Exercise 6.4: Eye Swings

We make great demands on our eyes in both work and recreation, particularly with all the time we spend with our computers and smartphones. Rarely do we think about our eyes unless they become a problem. However, eyes, like other parts of the body, can be relaxed and freed from rigid patterns. Viable methods for training and improving vision were developed and used in yoga traditions. Here we include some exercises that will help you to become more relaxed in your eyes, to open the way for better seeing and prepare you for the next series of exercises in attention to what you see.

Stand comfortably, weight balanced evenly between your two feet with your arms at your sides. Begin to swing your arms around from one side of your body to the other. Allow your body to twist gently with your arms, pivoting your feet as well. Let your head turn along with your body. As you make each swing, keep your eyes straight ahead and relaxed, so that your field of vision moves as you move. Your surroundings will seem to rush past you. Do not stop your head from flowing with the movement. After several minutes of pivots, back and forth, your eyes will feel looser.

Exercise 6.5: Eye Palming

The eyes can become very tired, and this tension carries through your whole body. Palming can relieve and relax your eyes.

Sit or lie down comfortably. Close your eyes. Place your palms very lightly on your face, touching your eye sockets. Do not press against your eyes. Your fingers can rest lightly on the top of your forehead, across each other, so that one is over, one under. Do not press. Rest for several minutes. Allow your eyes to relax beneath your palms. Let go of any unnecessary tension you might notice. After a comfortable time, remove your palms.

Exercise 6.6: Truly Seeing

Now that your eyes are relaxed, pick something that interests you as an object to look at. It could be a painting on the wall, a sculpture, a plant, a piece of furniture, or even an electronic device like a smartphone. Sit comfortably as you focus your attention on this object. Let your eyes move all around it and notice everything about it: texture, color, shape, and size. Allow yourself to be curious to see this object clearly, noticing what you see. If your mind wanders, gently bring it back to the object as soon as you notice that you have stopped looking. Keep focused on looking at the object and staying attuned to yourself as you look. In time, stop looking and relax your eyes again with swings or palming.

Practice this exercise as you are going about your day by taking a minute or two to truly see something in your environment. You may be surprised that this exercise enhances your memory for that object as you truly get to know it better through your sense of vision.

DEVELOPING YOUR OTHER SENSES: LISTENING, TASTING, AND SMELLING

All of your senses contribute to your experience. But you may tend to ignore some of senses and emphasize others. This may be part of your lifestyle. For example, a connoisseur of wine has a sensitive palate and can discern tastes and textures that other wine drinkers, who just like to drink it, might miss. These exercises are designed to attune you to other senses. Feel free to vary these exercises in creative ways. You will enrich the quality of your everyday experiencing, much as the client in our story did, adding depth and enhancing potential for your life.

Exercise 6.7: Sensing Sound: Listening as You Speak

You are often talking with others, but how often do you really listen to the sound of your own voice as you speak? Although you might feel silly if you are sitting by yourself, begin speaking aloud. Just say whatever comes to mind for 30 seconds or so, but as you do, listen! Hear the sound of your voice: Listen to the tones, the pauses, and the cadence.

Next, close your eyes and speak again, listening to the sound of your voice once more. Do you find it easier or more difficult to hear with your eyes closed? Your answer to this question will give you some clues for how to find your way into meditation most easily. We all have our natural tendencies, and it is helpful to get to know yours as you discover your best pathway into the experience.

For one more variation, cover your ears and speak again. You may notice that you hear your own voice clearly, but any outside sounds disappear. Listen for a minute or so, and notice what you hear. Then uncover your ears and compare as you speak again.

Exercise 6.8: Deep Listening

You probably have some music that you especially enjoy. Listen to it now, but with a difference. Deliberately keep your attention directed to the sound of the music. Listen carefully to the instruments as they express the melody. If the song has words, keep your attention on the sound of the words instead of their meaning. Hear the harmony, the flow of sounds. Let your body move with the song if you feel like doing so. Keep all your attention on the song, from beginning to end. If you find yourself thinking about something else, stop the song, and begin it again when your focus has returned to the song. Keep listening deeply, and enjoy the experience.

Exercise 6.9: Active Tasting

Everyone enjoys a delicious meal, but you may not be enjoying the taste of your food as much as you could. Take a moment to truly taste a food that you especially like. We often suggest eating a piece of fruit, but pick something that you like to eat. Begin slowly, and take one bite. Chew it all the way down, focused on tasting as you do. Eat slowly with awareness. If your mind drifts, stop eating and refocus your attention back on the food. Continue in this way until you have finished eating. Then sit for a moment and savor the taste in your mouth for a moment or two.

Exercise 6.10: Noticing Aromas

Find an aromatic plant or light a bit of incense. Sit down nearby and turn your attention to the smells. Close your eyes. Notice the qualities of the fragrance as you breathe in a relaxed way. Keep focused on the scent for several minutes. Take time in your day, a minute here or there, to notice the aromas around you. They are always there, but people often do not take the time to notice them.

INTEROCEPTION: INTERNAL BODY SENSING

You can attune to your internal body experiencing directly by paying attention to breathing, heartbeat, or pulse. Here are some ways to attend to inner sensory sensations. You will find other exercises in later chapters of this book as well.

Exercise 6.11: First Step to Breathing Awareness

Breathing is part of every great meditation tradition, and we offer many breathing meditations throughout this book.

Introduce yourself to the process now by placing your hands lightly on your rib cage. Then breathe normally as you experience the movement that accompanies each breath. Keep your breathing natural and comfortable. Close your eyes if it helps you to sense the movement of each breath more vividly.

Exercise 6.12: Pulse Awareness

You can find your pulse easily by placing the tips of your index and middle finger over the inner wrist on the thumb side, right inside your wrist. Move your fingers around slightly until you feel the pulse. Then hold them there, close your eyes, and pay attention to the quality, speed, and sensations you feel there. Sit calmly as you notice these sensory experiences, which reflect your internal body functioning. Perform this exercise at different times of the day and in different environments. The ancient healers of China could diagnose bodily states simply by feeling the pulse of their patients; in a sense, they were listening to the inner being of the patient through touch. As you become more attuned to your own internal experiences, you may begin to notice distinct changes in the qualities of your pulse associated with different circumstances.

Exercise 6.13: Heartbeat Awareness

You can even attune to deep internal processes such as heartbeat if you take the time to pay attention. Find a quiet place to get in touch with the subtle body experience of the beating of your own heart. You probably have felt your heartbeat after running fast or when feeling afraid, but the sounds and sensations are fainter when you are sitting quietly. Place your hand over your heart area, and close your eyes. Allow yourself to sense the beating of your heart. You will feel a slight movement and hear a subtle sound. Stay attuned to this internal body experience as you relax and breathe comfortably.

CONCLUSION

Take time each day to stop for a moment of sensory awareness. Turn your attention to each sense separately, then take a few minutes to open to all your sensing. As you enhance your sensory experiencing, you will notice more, be aware of your embodied experiencing and become in touch with your environment, thereby enriching the quality of your life.

7

Body Movement and the Mind–Body Link

Core Principle 7: The Mind and Body Are Linked. Meditative Movement of the Body Can Elicit a Meditative State of Mind.

A book on cooking will not cure hunger. To feel satisfied we must have actual food. So long as we do not go beyond mere talking, we are not true knowers.

— Suzuki

INTRODUCTION

Meditative movement may help your clients to taste their meditative experience more completely. Meditation is not something that must be restricted to just sitting still. Rather, it is a quality of awareness and an attitude that persists all through the day's activities. Thus, meditation is a combination of stillness and movement, where appropriate.

Thoughts and feelings take place through and in the body. When you are angry, your face might flush, and your breathing rate increases. Love makes your heart race and perhaps your skin tingle. Thoughts elicit body experiences as well. Just thinking about a funny joke might bring an automatic smile to your face. Eastern traditions have long recognized the deep interconnection of mind and body, and neuroscience confirms this link. As neuroscientists, we emphasize that we are embodied cognition.

The nervous system extends through the whole body, connecting to the brain (see Figure 7.1). And so, through your thoughts and emotions, you

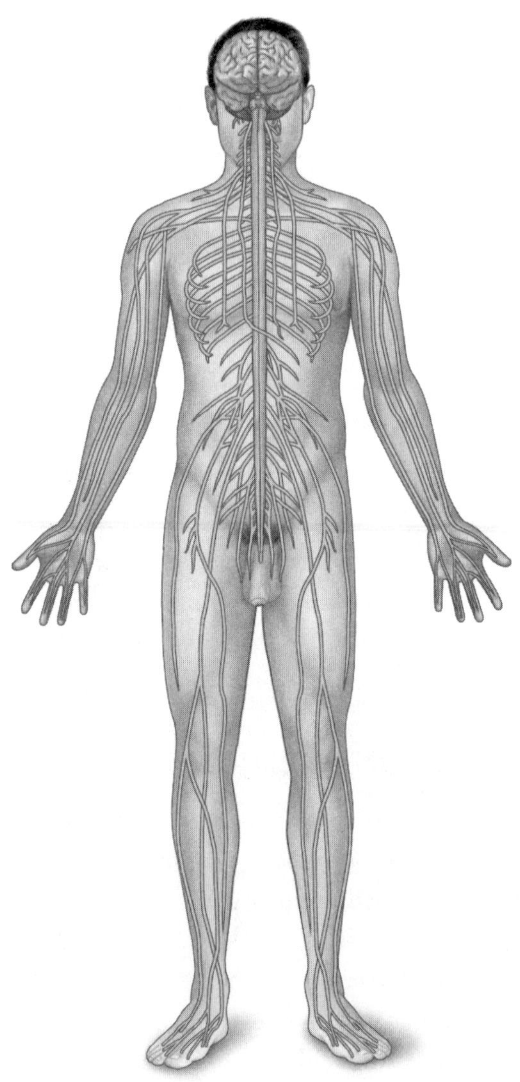

Figure 7.1   Central Nervous System

can influence your body just as you can affect your body in many ways with your thoughts and emotions. This understanding allows you to add a new dimension to therapy by working with body meditations.

Many meditation traditions include body positioning and movement as a path to higher consciousness. Yoga uses postures, known as asanas. Tai Chi incorporates flowing, soft movements. Qigong has poses and movements of its own. These meditative poses, postures, and movements enhance mind-body unity. And they have a direct influence on brain functions, helping to calm and balance the nervous system. Recent research finds the meditative movement is different from conventional exercise. By viewing Eastern conceptions such as moving the internal energy (chi) in terms of the physiological effects on the brain functions and electrical activity of the nervous system, we can understand why moving meditations are so helpful for therapy (Payne & Crane-Godreau, 2013). By engaging the body as part of meditation, you learn to enhance harmony within your embodied nature.

This chapter explains the neuroscience of movement, which shows why moving meditations are so powerful. You will observe the mind-brain-body connection, known as the ideomotor link, in action, and learn exercises for experiencing and using it. And through the meditative practices that you learn, you will foster the mind-body connection, which brings experiences of harmony and peace for you and your clients.

MOVEMENT IS REGULATED BY MANY BRAIN AREAS, FROM TOP DOWN AND BOTTOM UP

Body movement is central to our functioning. Its importance is reflected by its prominence all through the nervous system. We have the ability to move built in, interconnected with our emotions and thoughts. We may move deliberately. For example, when you want to stretch, the motor cortex in your frontal lobes activates, communicating with structures in the center of your brain, including the basal ganglia, to send signals down into the lower areas, the cerebellum and brain stem, to regulate movements. Also, we may move without thought. For example, when you sit down in a comfortable chair, you often feel yourself relax spontaneously. This spontaneous movement response is regulated bottom up, coming from the lower brain areas, which send a signal to let go of tension.

Both of these motor processes release dopamine, the neurotransmitter that helps to regulate movement. Dopamine is also the neurotransmitter involved when you feel pleasure, reward, and enjoyment. As you have certainly experienced, when you have been sitting still for a long time and then stand up to walk around, moving feels good. Moving meditations not only help you to regulate your emotions; they bring feelings of well-being.

THE MECHANISM THAT LINKS MIND AND MOVEMENT: THE IDEOMOTOR RESPONSE

Nervous system activity consists of two parts: a sensory experience and a motor action. The somatic nervous system carries the sensory inputs to the brain and then translates these signals into motor outputs. You can activate this natural, automatic interaction between mind and body deliberately to what William James, one of the founding fathers of modern psychology, called the ideomotor response. The ideomotor response proceeds from having a sensory input or an idea that is translated into a bodily response. The signal travels from your thought as an input, directly to the nervous system, which illustrates how intimately linked our mind and body really are. You can tap into this natural capacity to elicit an ideomotor response through meditation for balance and calm.

Exercise 7.1: Eliciting an Ideosensory Response

If you would like to experience the power of the ideomotor effect, close your eyes and imagine a tart lemon. Think about the yellow pulp, the lemony aroma. Then imagine placing a piece in your mouth. Taste the tart flavor. Does your mouth begin to water? If so, you have experienced the ideomotor link between mind and body: An imagined image becomes directly expressed in the body response.

Exercise 7.2: Producing the Ideomotor Response

This exercise uses the imagination of movement, which is translated into real movement in your hand.

Get a plumb bob, ring, or any small, object with some weight. Attach it to a string. Hold the string from the top and let the object dangle freely.

Hold your arm out in a relaxed way so that you are comfortable as you hold the string, leaving your arm and wrist free (see Figure 7.2). Now close your eyes. Imagine that the pendulum begins to swing back and forth in a certain direction. Picture it vividly in your mind. Do not deliberately move or interfere with the hand that holds the string. Instead, focus on your imaginative image of swinging. Visualize the rhythmic sweep of the swing becoming longer. After a few minutes, open your eyes and look at the pendulum. You probably will find that it is swinging back and forth as you imagined.

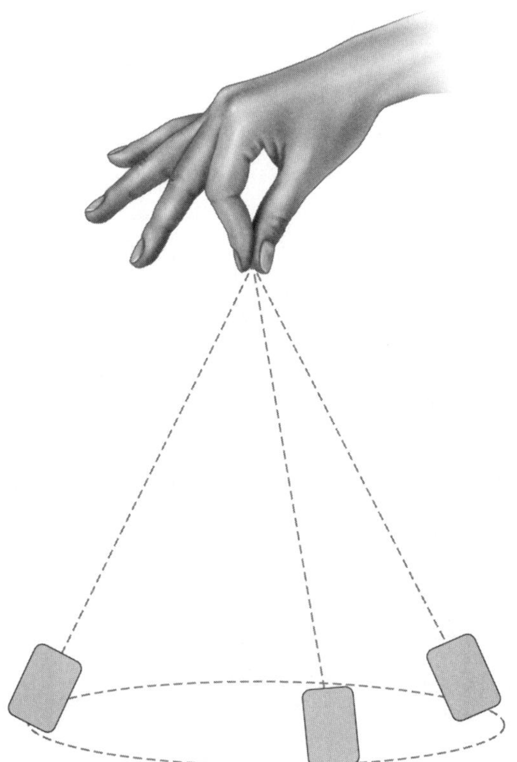

Figure 7.2   Ideomotor Pendulum Swinging

Close your eyes again. Visualize the object swinging in the other direction. Exaggerate the image so that the arc becomes larger and larger in the new direction. Picture it as vividly as possible. Once again, do not disturb the hand that holds the string. Simply focus on your visualization. After a time, open your eyes. Is the pendulum swinging in the new direction?

Close your eyes one last time. Imagine that the pendulum swings in a circle. Allow the circular orbit to become larger and larger. Open your eyes to check the movement of the pendulum. Large movements may take time and practice to develop further. Some people can do it almost immediately. Others expand their abilities over time.

Exercise 7.3: Ideomotor Relaxation

The ideomotor link shows you how your mind can bring about effects in your body just as your body affects your mind. Recalling a painful traumatic event and holding it in mind often inadvertently activates the ideomotor effect, leading to pain in the body. This effect helps to explain why people who are suffering from emotional pain often feel pain in the body as well.

You can cultivate the link to reverse this process and bring about positive relief of comfort and relaxation.

You can use the ideomotor effect to bring about your own relaxation and calm. Sit in a comfortable chair or lie down on the floor or a bed. Can you remember a time when you felt completely relaxed and at ease? Perhaps you were on a vacation or in the company of someone you care about, or maybe you were alone out in nature. Think of some experience you had when you felt really good. You may prefer to think about someone else being relaxed, such as your partner or your young child peacefully sleeping. Imagine this experience as vividly as possible. Recall what you saw, the sounds you heard, and what you felt in your body. Hold the image in mind for several minutes, and wait for your response. Your body will respond naturally. You will become calmer, like the image in your mind, without you trying to make it happen.

CENTERING

Psychotherapy often encourages clients to find their emotional center, to find balance in feeling and expression of emotion. This is often done using cognitive methods that help to moderate feelings through thoughts. The brain is working top down, activating the prefrontal cortex for thinking and the cingulate cortex, which regulates the emotional limbic system.

Some clients may find it easier to elicit emotional balance through a bottom-up experience of centering. This exercise works through the lower brain area movement centers to influence thoughts and feelings bottom up. The next two exercises elicit a sense of balance through the body.

Exercise 7.4: Body Centering

This series of instructions will help to discover a balanced standing posture, known in Yoga as the mountain pose, *tadasana*. Balance is discovered bottom up by attuning to alignment with gravity. From a centered position, standing becomes effortless. And through the process of discovering balance, emotions settle and thoughts clear.

Begin the process by standing with your feet together, ankles touching and arms at your sides. If you feel uncomfortable, you can move your feet slightly apart. Stand up straight without being stiff. Keep your shoulders from slumping, and don't let your back hunch. Look straight ahead, keeping your head upright and centered. Breathe comfortably and focus your attention on just standing.

Now move your legs slightly apart, approximately shoulder width. Place your weight evenly between your two feet. Rock gently from side to side, and feel your balance point shifting first to one leg and then to the other. Stop for a moment with your weight more on one foot and pay attention to how that side feels (see Figure 7.3). How long does it feel, from your ankle to the floor, from your knee to the floor, from your hip to the floor, and then from your shoulder to the floor? Without moving, turn your attention to the other leg that has less weight on it. Do you perceive the two legs differently? Now rock gently back and forth several times sideways. You will discover a place exactly between your two legs where balance is effortless and shared by both legs equally. Let yourself stand for a few moments as you sense this balance point between.

Next, try rocking very slightly forward and back. You will feel muscles tighten as a group when you shift forward and backward. Sense the length and breadth of the front of your body and compare that to the length and breadth of the back of your body. Now rock just a little, very gently, forward and backward. Notice the point in the middle where your muscles relax and your feet are resting on the ground. Just stand for a moment in that place between side to side and forward and backward, where you are most relaxed and balanced, aligned with gravity: centered.

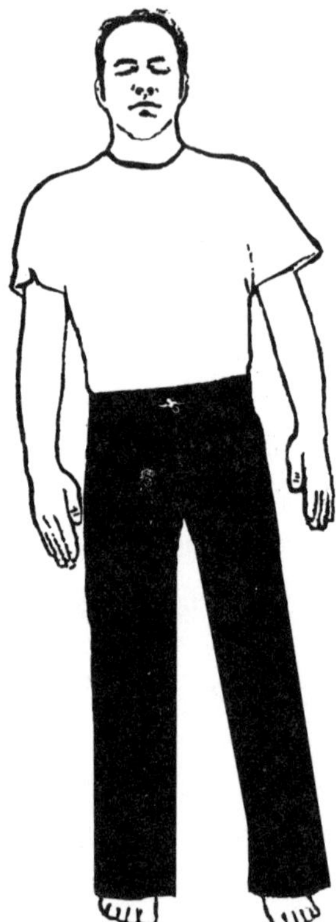

Figure 7.3   Shifting Weight

Exercise 7.5: Centering through Nostril Breathing

Breathing is another gateway to emotions through the body. Control of the breath can influence thoughts and emotions, so learning to work with the breath can have a strong influence on your psychological adjustment.

How can breathing have such a profound effect on experiencing? Breathing links the lungs with the heart and stomach through the vagus nerve, the tenth of the 12 cranial nerves in the nervous system. The vagus nerve is linked directly to the parasympathetic nervous system, the part of the autonomic nervous system that calms the body and helps it return to balance following sympathetic nervous system activation from fear or stress. Research shows that by doing certain kinds of breathing meditations, you activate the vagus nerve (Porges, 2011). Activating the vagus nerve lowers stress, and breathing meditations help make this happen.

Breathing through both nostrils evenly has been shown to activate the vagus nerve. This nostril breathing exercise brings you to balance by opening both nostrils to take in and expel air evenly. Typically, as you go through your day, you breathe more out of one nostril or the other. You can hold a mirror up under your nose to see the moisture of your breath coming from one side. The nostril side oxygenates its opposite side of the brain, so that when you breathe from your left nostril, you are activating your right hemisphere. Breathing from both nostrils simultaneously tends to oxygenate the whole brain for alert attention while also eliciting a calm balance.

Practice the next meditation for 5 to 10 minutes. Repeat it at various times through the day, especially when you feel the need for calm.

Begin by curling your fingers of your left hand as you hold your left thumb out. Place your left thumb over your left nostril and inhale, exhale, and inhale again out of the open right nostril (Figure 7.4). Then use the side of your bent index finger to close your right nostril as you remove your thumb from the left nostril and exhale, inhale, and exhale (Figure 7.5). Without pause, slide your

Figure 7.4   Nostril Breathing 1

Figure 7.5   Nostril Breathing 2

thumb over your left nostril again and repeat the pattern. Move from one nostril to the other in this way. Repeat the pattern for several minutes. Then breathe out of both nostrils together. You will experience openness and balance in your breathing and an overall sense of energy and emotional balance.

MOVING MEDITATIONS

When performing any of these moving meditations, keep your mind focused on your movements and your breathing. Relax any unnecessary tensions to allow your body to move gently back and forth, without forcing a movement farther than is comfortable. Don't force yourself to take deep breaths either, just breathe comfortably as you move. Be patient and persistent for the best results. With breath and movement united, you will free the flow of energy to help you find calm and balance.

Exercise 7.6: Eight Pieces of Brocade

One of the moving meditation traditions from China, Qigong, involves doing sets of movements by tensing and relaxing muscles that coordinate with the breath. Research on Qigong shows that, as with yoga, practice results in a decrease in anxiety and stress by affecting the hypothalamic-pituitary-adrenal axis pathway (Lee, Kang, Lim, & Lee, 2004). And it also has been shown to help with pain and moods (Yang, Kim, & Lee, 2005).

This particular Qigong series is based on the series known as the Eight Pieces of Brocade. These exercises date back to the Sung Dynasty (960–1279) in China. Brocade is a cloth of great beauty and value with finely woven patterns. These gentle exercises are beautiful patterns that have value for enhancing health and well-being.

Stand quietly for a few minutes. Let your breathing become calm and natural. Keep your back relatively straight. Perform the movements slowly, keeping your body relaxed. Hold each pose for a minute or two, and increase the time for each pose if it feels comfortable to do so. Repeat each exercise three to five times and then proceed to the next one. Continue until you have done all eight.

These eight exercises, performed in sequence, activate the entire body. Be sure to keep your attention fully focused on the movement, as the mind is an important component for raising your chi. You will begin to feel a slight change in energy, experienced as warmth or tingling.

Piece One: Stand with your feet shoulder width apart, hands dropped straight down at your sides (Figure 7.6a). Exhaling, rotate your head to the left without straining (Figure 7.6b). Keep the rest of your body still. Inhale as you bring your head back to face front, then exhale again as you turn your head to the right. Finally inhale while you turn to face front.

Piece Two: Intertwine your fingers together with palms facing out (see Figure 7.7a) and then carefully swing your arms up over your head as you exhale (see Figure 7.7b). As you inhale, bring your hands back down in front of your body (see Figure 7.7c).

Figure 7.6a   Piece One

Figure 7.6b   Piece One

Figure 7.7a   Piece Two

Figure 7.7b   Piece Two

Figure 7.7c   Piece Two

Piece Three: Place your hands palm up in front of your body, elbows bent and fingertips touching (see Figure 7.8a). As you exhale, move your left hand up over your head with your palm facing up as you simultaneously move your right hand down in front, palm down (see Figure 7.8b). As you inhale, return your hands to their original position. Then exhale as you reverse, raising the right hand overhead, palm up, and the left hand down, palm down.

Piece Four: Begin with your fists held at your waist, palms facing up. While you inhale, step to the left into a slightly wider stance, known in martial arts as the horse stance. Let your knees bend slightly (see Figure 7.9a). Exhale and turn your body to the left. Cross your arms out to the left side, both hands in a fist (see Figure 7.9b). Inhale and open your left hand, palm facing away from you, as you draw your right hand, still in a fist, back to your chest, as if getting ready to shoot an arrow (see Figure 7.9c). Then exhale and return to face front, drawing both fists to your waist in coordination with left foot drawing back to shoulder

Figure 7.8a   Piece Three

Figure 7.8b   Piece Three

Figure 7.9a   Piece Four

Figure 7.9b   Piece Four

Figure 7.9c   Piece Four

width (see Figure 7.9a). Pivot to the right and repeat the pattern as you exhale, stepping out to the right, extending both hands to the right, and pulling back the bow. Turn back to face front while inhaling.

Piece Five: Step to the left into the horse stance. Let your hands rest on your thighs (see Figure 7.10a). Exhale and lean to the left without raising your feet (see Figure 7.10b). Inhale as you return to center (see Figure 7.10a). Exhale while you lean to the right. Inhale as you return to center.

Piece Six: Bring your legs back to shoulder width apart. Raise your hands, palms up, fingers touching, as in Piece Three (see Figure 7.11a). Then gently stretch forward as you exhale, directing palms down to the floor with fingers facing each other (see Figure 7.11b). Don't try to go farther than you can comfortably. Gradually, flexibility will increase. Inhale while returning to standing (see Figure 7.11a).

Figure 7.10a　Piece Five

Figure 7.10b　Piece Five

Figure 7.11a   Piece Six

Figure 7.11b   Piece Six

Piece Seven: From a horse stance position with fists at your sides (see Figure 7.12a), turn your head to the left and watch as you slowly and gently punch with the left fist to the left, exhaling as your fist moves outward (see Figure 7.12b). Inhale as you return to the original position (see Figure 7.12a). Then turn your head to watch as you slowly and gently punch to the right with the right fist while exhaling. Inhale as you return to center in the original position.

Piece Eight: For the final piece, stand with your feet together, hands at your sides. Keep your legs straight (see Figure 7.13a). Inhale while rising up on your toes (see Figure 7.13 b & c). Exhale slowly while lowering your heels (see Figure 7.13a).

Figure 7.12a   Piece Seven

Figure 7.12b   Piece Seven

Figure 7.13a   Piece Eight

Figure 7.13b   Piece Eight

Figure 7.13c   Piece Eight

Exercise 7.7: Bottom-up Calming with the Sun Salutation

Many of your clients will be familiar with yoga, and so adding some yoga postures into your treatment plan can have a powerful effect. You can use the sun's function of giving energy to the world as a symbol for energizing the entire body through the practice of the sun salutation. The dynamic movements reach from head to toe and are balanced, with forward and backward bending. Breathing is combined with movements to help you develop control and calm. This series can help in losing weight, massaging the digestive system, and regulating circulation. And the regular practice leads to feelings of well-being.

The sun salutation is performed in slow, continuous motion. You can repeat the entire series several times, up to ten times each day, but two to three times is usual, especially if you do it daily.

Coordinate breathing with each move in the following way: Breathe in when you arch your back or stretch. Breathe out when you bend forward or contract. Make your breaths and your movements slow and continuous. Keep attention on what you are doing as you synchronize your breathing with your movements. You may experience an uplifting union of mind with body. Allow yourself to enjoy the experience.

Before you begin, warm up your body for a few minutes with a few gentle stretches, arm swings, and raising and lowering your legs. Once you feel limber and relaxed, begin performing the sun salutation.

1. *Opening Position* (see Figure 7.14): Stand straight in mountain pose, with your feet together, chest lifted, shoulders square, and neck lengthened. Bend your elbows and hold the palms of your hands together, thumbs touching, at the center of your chest. Keep your weight evenly distributed between your two feet. Close your eyes and breathe in and out several times, centering yourself in your body experience in the moment.

2. *Upright Arch* (see Figure 7.15): Open your eyes and inhale as you stretch your arms up over your head, palms facing each other. Arch back as you push your hips out, keeping your legs straight. Gently relax your neck back. Begin to arch from your upper back rather than the lower back. Arch slowly and carefully.

Figure 7.14 Opening Position

3. *Forward Bend* (see Figures 7.16a and 7.16b): Next exhale as you slowly bend forward, keeping your arms extended. Move your arms and upper body downward, bending at the waist, toward the floor. Keep your back straight for as long as possible as you go down (see Figure 7.16a). Let your neck relax and your head hang down. Bring your fingertips down to your toes, and bend your knees slightly if needed (see Figure 7.16b). Hold the position briefly as you relax fully into the forward stretch.

4. *Lunging Arch* (see Figure 7.17): Inhale as you extend your left leg back approximately four feet behind your right, allowing your left knee to rest on the floor. Your right foot rests flat on the floor with your knee bent. Let your hands rest on the floor at your sides to steady this motion. Then raise your arms up overhead, arch your back, and look up toward the sun. If you feel shaky in your balance, keep your hands on the floor

Figure 7.15   Upright Arch

Figure 7.16a   Forward Bend

Figure 7.16b   Forward Bend

Figure 7.17   Lunging Arch

at your sides as you arch. Hold the position briefly, allowing your upper body to stretch backward as much as is comfortable.

5. *Dog Pose* (see Figure 7.18): Exhaling, bring your left foot back next to the right. Lift your hips up as high as you can as you place your hands, palms down, on the floor extended out in front of you. Expand your chest as you relax your neck and look down between your hands. Push your heels toward the floor, and feel a gentle stretch.

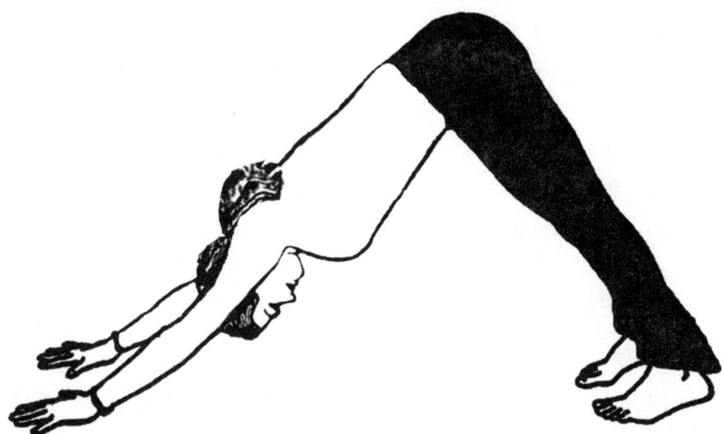

Figure 7.18   Dog Pose

6. *Cobra Stretch* (see Figure 7.19): Next lower yourself facedown to the floor and inhale as you arch and draw the upper body slowly up, but not to a point of pain, vertebrae by vertebrae, beginning at your lower back and

Figure 7.19   Cobra Stretch

moving upward. Stop if there is pain, and lower your upper body gently to rest on the floor again. Never force the exercise. As you get to the neck area, allow your head to arch back slowly until you achieve a full upper-body stretch.

7. Now you are half way around the series of movements. The second half of the sun salutation is to repeat all the same motions in reverse on the opposite side. Following the cobra pose, perform the dog pose as you exhale. Then lunge back with your right leg as you inhale and smoothly arch back with your upper body. Exhale as you bring your right leg back to your left and lift your hips up as you bend your upper body down, bringing your head toward your knees. Straighten your upper body up and lift your arms overhead to stretch backward as you inhale. End as you began, with your arms returning to the position at your chest, palms and thumbs touching. Then pause, close your eyes, and pay attention to your feelings as you sense the effects of the sun salutation. Meditate for a moment in this position, then begin again.

ELICITING CHANGE THROUGH BODY POSITIONING

Attitudes and feelings are expressed in how you hold your body. If you are feeling self-confident, you tend to stand upright, with shoulders squared and rib cage lifted, whereas when you are feeling insecure or frightened, you might hunch forward or look down. The effect can be reciprocal. So, by altering your posture, you can elicit a different emotional experience. Use the warrior pose to elicit feelings of confidence, the child pose to elicit feelings of security and self-soothing, and the triangle pose to feel more flexible. Many other poses also can elicit helpful feelings. Now that you understand the principle of using postures to elicit an emotional state, we encourage you to experiment to find what works best for you.

Exercise 7.8: Taking a Confident Stance in the Warrior Pose

Confidence is reflected in how you hold your body. The warrior pose (see Figure 7.20) develops strength in the feet, arches, calves, and thighs. It also works the abdomen and shoulders. The position is symbolic of

Figure 7.20   Warrior Pose

taking a strong stand, and you will feel your strength build as you embody it through this posture.

Begin by stepping out approximately three feet. Bend your right front knee, keeping the lower leg perpendicular, with the thigh parallel to the floor so that the bent leg forms as close to a 90-degree angle as possible. Keep your hips level. As you move into the foot position, bring your arms up overhead. Then spread your arms out from your sides, directly over your legs, parallel to the floor with fingers held together and pointing straight out. Turn your head to face the forward bent leg, keeping your neck and back straight. Lift your chest and stretch out through your arms and fingers (see Figure 7.20). Hold the position as you breathe in and out for as long as you can without discomfort.

Move slowly in and out of each position, keeping your motions smooth. Hold each position as long as you can, breathing in and out, and then move slowly into the other side position, facing in the opposite direction.

Exercise 7.9: Self-Soothing and Feeling Secure: The Child Pose

The child pose (see Figure 7.21) offers a feeling of self-support that can be reassuring, especially after dealing with disturbing emotions.

Figure 7.21   Child Pose

Go into a kneeling position and then sit down with your feet tucked under you. Bend forward slowly until your head touches the floor. Allow your arms to rest comfortably at your sides with your elbows bent so that they can rest on the floor (see Figure 7.21). You may need to shift or move slightly to find the most comfortable position. Adjust your breathing to a calm rhythm, and rest in this position.

Exercise 7.10: Flexibility with the Triangle Pose

The body may become rigid and inflexible, to express a narrow, rigid attitude. You can start the process of loosening the hold of rigidity by the simple act of stretching your body.

Perform each posture in the triangle pose (see Figure 7.22) slowly, with your mind fully focused during every movement. Don't force the stretch, and only go as far as you can comfortably. Pay attention to the subtle differences in tension and relaxation of various muscles. Observe sensations and positioning. Notice how your breathing affects your body positioning. If you stay fully attentive and do not ignore your body's counterreactions, you will derive deep benefit. From the simple comes the profound.

Place your legs approximately two feet apart, raise your arms out sideways to shoulder height, and inhale. Slowly bend to the left, keeping your arms stretched out, and begin exhaling. Rotate your left hand down to lightly grasp your left leg as the right arm comes overhead until it is pointing straight up as you continue to bend sideways. From this position, relax your neck muscles and any other muscles

Figure 7.22   Triangle Pose

that are not involved in this stretch. Breathe comfortably (see Figure 7.22). Slowly straighten as you inhale again and return to the starting position. Repeat the same motion on the other side.

CONCLUSION

Include the body in meditation in order to enhance therapy. You can activate responsiveness directly, bottom up, thereby bypassing some of the resistances to change. By doing so you will encourage positive emotions that will help heal emotional wounds and help to bring about a healthier and happier adjustment.

PART IV

MEDITATION INSTRUCTIONS

8

Focus Meditations

Core Principle 8: Narrow Your Focus to Cultivate Stability, Regulation, Tranquility, and Self-Control.

When the agitations of the mind are under control, the mind becomes like a transparent crystal and has the power of becoming whatever form is presented, knower, act of knowing, or what is known.

—*Patanjali,* The Yoga Sutras

INTRODUCTION

At a fundamental level, many of our clients suffer from an inability to harness the mind. Troubling thoughts and feelings bombard them, leaving many to feel desperate and out of control. Focusing is one of the three fundamental meditative skills that can train clients to retake the reins and find peace of mind.

Yoga has a long tradition of teaching how to direct attention at will. This chapter includes instructions, drawn from this long-lived meditation tradition for how to focus and keep focus steady. This chapter instructs in focus meditations that teach how to direct attention toward one thing or else away from one thing at will. Clients will benefit from developing these skills in many specific and nonspecific ways. For some, learning how to hold the mind steady fills a deficit. Others, who are too narrowly focused on problems and disturbance, can be gently guided to redirect their focus toward something more realistic or even more positive.

Exercise 8.1: Narrowing Attention

People often have difficulty focusing on something because their attention becomes distracted. You can cultivate the ability to focus by the practice of deliberately withdrawing attention from outer stimuli. This exercise, drawn from the great yoga tradition of pratyahara, turns attention away from the outer world to focus it inward.

Sit comfortably and quietly for a few moments. Then notice everything around you: the sounds around you, the temperature of the air, any aromas, and the quality of the light in the room where you are sitting. Focus on everything surrounding you for several minutes.

Next, turn your attention to whatever is close to you, such as the feeling of your clothing, smooth or textured, loose or tight. Notice the chair you are sitting on, whether it feels hard or soft, warm or cool. How do your feet meet the floor: Are they resting lightly on the floor or pushing against it? Keep your attention focused on what is close to you for several minutes.

Now notice inner body sensations. Scan through your body to notice your muscles. Are you holding them tight, or are your muscles relaxed? Is there any unnecessary tightening? If possible, relax any tensions that can be relaxed. Turn your attention to your breathing. Allow it to be natural as you notice how the breath goes in through your nose and then out again. Perhaps you can sense your pulse or heartbeat.

Finally, withdraw attention from your body sensations to focus on your thoughts. Notice the thoughts as if you are sitting on the bank of a river, watching each thought float by. If your attention wanders back to inner sensations, to other stimuli close to you, or to something else in the outer environment, gently bring attention back to your thoughts as soon as you can. Maintain the focus for several minutes. The ability to withdraw your attention from distractions responds to practice, so repeat this exercise in different rooms of the house or even outdoors.

Exercise 8.2: Holding Attention

Once attention has been narrowed, it can be trained to remain steadily directed to one thing. Deliberately focusing will help you gain better control. This can become a great resource. Do this exercise, which builds on the attention exercises in Chapter 5, with clients who may be having trouble focusing attention.

Now begin to focus on one thing. Pick an object, picture, or piece of art that is interesting to your client. It may be a fascinating piece of art in your office. A teenage client might be more interested in focusing on technology, and a child might prefer a stuffed animal or cartoon picture. Place the object in clear view.

Sit upright cross-legged on the floor, on a small pillow, or on a straight-backed chair, and look at the object. Keep your attention on it, and notice as many aspects of the object that you can see such as the shapes, patterns, sizes, and even their meaning to you. If your attention wanders away, where does it go? If possible, retrace the links back to the object of focus. Begin with just two or three minutes. Gradually increase the time as you become able to maintain your concentration. You will improve with practice.

Exercise 8.3: Focusing on an Inner Image

Attention can be focused on outer objects, but it can also be directed inwards and kept focused there. This exercise teaches how to direct attention inwards and hold it on an inner image, a useful skill for psychotherapy.

After directing your attention to an object with your eyes open, close your eyes and picture the image within. People who are naturally able to form visual pictures will see a vivid image of the object. For others, the picture may be vague. Keep your attention focused on the image even if the imagined image is vague. Notice all the details that you saw when looking at the object, such as the patterns and shapes. If you find that you have forgotten some of the details, open your eyes to look again. Notice more about the object, then close your eyes again and visualize the picture as an inner image. Keep switching between eyes opened to look and eyes closed to visualize for several minutes until you feel that you are able to hold a clear sense of the object within.

Exercise 8.4: One-Pointed Awareness

The ability to direct attention to a single point and keep it there is a classic way to enter a deep meditative state. The skill can be trained with practice. Directing attention in this way is a valuable ability for therapy when you need to become aware of inner concerns and experiences, even if they are uncomfortable. And when learning something new, one-pointed awareness can make the learning process flow smoothly. This exercise develops this useful one-pointed awareness skill.

An easy place to begin is by focusing attention on a color. Pick your favorite color. Once you have chosen, close your eyes and think about the color. You might find it easier to see the color fill your perceptual field, the screen of your mind, or you might prefer to think of something specific of that color, such as a blue sky, a large green chalkboard, or an enormous yellow sun. Keep your attention directed to the color and only that color. If another thought or other object of interest emerges, gently let it go and return to focusing on the color. Begin focusing attention for as few as 30 seconds if you are working with young children or clients who have a short attention span, and gradually increase the time to between two and five minutes. This skill improves dramatically with practice. You will enjoy the experience of control and calm that results.

Exercise 8.5: Flexible Variations

Think of your favorite color for several minutes. Once you have done so, imagine that it becomes smaller and smaller, until it shrinks down to a single concentrated dot. Then let it become larger and larger again. For a variation, let the shape change from a square to a circle or a triangle. You might enjoy allowing the color to change into another color or even become a rainbow of colors. Be playful with the shifting. You can have fun with this exercise, allowing imagination to alter the image in many creative ways.

FOCUS ON BREATHING

Meditation has long recognized the power of the breath and has many methods for developing it. The ability to maintain your attention on breathing teaches the broader skill of directing focus to any object of choice.

Some of your clients will do well with focusing on an image, but for others, visualizing does not come naturally. These clients may relate better to focusing on the body. Breathing is a natural way to focus attention on a body experience. And focusing on breathing can help form a bridge to moods and emotions. Methods of meditative breathing have been taught for thousands of years.

Neuroscience now has revealed how breathing is intimately linked to the lungs, heart, stomach, and brain (Porges, 2011). By becoming aware and working with the breath through meditation, you can promote health by calming all these body areas and also calming mental activity as well (Jerath, Edry, Bames, & Jerath, 2006). And when attention is focused on breathing, you will enhance meditation skills.

Exercise 8.6: Bringing Attention from Outside to Inside

This exercise is especially helpful for people who have difficulty turning their attention inward.

Breathe normally and comfortably. Place your hands low on your rib cage, and close your eyes. Turn your attention to the movement of your hands. Feel how your hands move slightly in and out, up and down as you breathe. Keep your attention focused on the movement. As you do, you will find it easy to notice each breath, in and out.

Exercise 8.7: Counting the Breaths

Now that you have felt your breaths move your rib cage in and out, practice counting the breaths. By engaging in the count, most people will be able to keep their attention focused on breathing for several minutes. We have found this to be a favorite exercise of children as well.

Sit comfortably in a way that allows your breathing passages to be free. Don't slouch down, but also don't hold yourself rigidly upright either. Just sit up relatively straight and comfortably. Breathe through your nose as you normally do when sitting quietly. Inwardly count each complete breath, in and out. Beginning with 1, count each breath up to 10. Breathe normally, without trying to change anything. When you get to 10, start over in your count, and go up to 10 again. Remember not to breathe harder or faster—just breathe normally, and count every breath. If your thoughts wander away from counting, gently bring yourself back to counting as soon as you notice. Keep counting for several minutes. When you are finished, open your eyes, and stand up and stretch.

Exercise 8.8: Following the Breath

For this exercise, sit cross-legged on a pillow or on a chair, or you can lie down on the floor on your back. Most important is to allow your breathing passages to be relatively relaxed. Breathe through your nose, not your mouth. Close your eyes and turn your attention to your breathing. Notice the air as it comes in through your nose, then flows down into your lungs and then out again. Pay close attention to how your chest, diaphragm, stomach, and back move as you breathe. Don't interfere with the natural pattern of breathing. Just relax and breathe normally as you keep your attention focused on the process of breathing. If your attention wanders, gently bring it back to focus on breathing. For those who find this exercise difficult to do, return to breath-counting exercise. These skills improve with practice, so keep trying.

USING FOCUS MEDITATION THERAPEUTICALLY

You have probably had the experience of asking your client, "What do you feel?" and received the answer, "Oh, I think I'm good," or "I'm just awful!" Some people have difficulty attuning to feelings. They refer to them abstractly in terms of thoughts *about* them. Focusing on breathing can help people get in touch with their emotions because breathing is so intimately linked to feelings. Whenever we feel an emotion, our breathing changes. For this reason, attending to breathing can become an inroad to emotional awareness. And so, by turning your clients' focus to their breathing, you can help them to become more in touch with their emotional experiencing. As a therapist, you can also learn more about your clients' emotions by observing the quality of their breath. Use the exercises below to help your clients work with emotions through breathing meditation.

Exercise 8.9: Awareness of Feelings

When you are feeling a certain emotion, take a moment to sit down and focus your attention on breathing. Notice the rhythm of your breath. Is it fast or slow? What is its quality: Is it pushed, labored, shallow, or perhaps deep? Pay attention to surrounding muscles in your rib cage, neck, face, and back. Do you perceive patterns of tension? Discern any other sensations that accompany your breathing, such as heat or cold, tingling or numbness. Also, note what thoughts you are having. If you would like to alter the feeling, sit a little longer and try some of the previous exercises for permitting, relaxing, or controlling the breath. You may feel the emotion begin to subside slightly.

Later, repeat this exercise when you are having a different feeling. Compare and contrast the quality of breathing with different emotions. Getting to know what your breathing is like when you have different feelings and moods may be helpful for bringing about change.

Exercise 8.10: Regulating Your Feelings Naturally through Movement with Breathing

When people suffer from anxiety, they may find that sitting still to focus their attention makes them more anxious. You can introduce movement into the exercise to help allay anxiety while still bringing about regulation of emotion. The quality of attention is what matters; focusing on the coordination of movement with breathing can have a calming effect.

Close your eyes and then turn your attention to your breathing. Listen to the sound as the air goes in through your nose and down into your lungs. Allow your rib cage and chest to expand and then return to rest as you exhale. Let breathing be as natural and relaxed as possible, without forcing it. Keep listening to the sound of your breathing, in and out, for several minutes. Then raise your hands, palms facing up, as you inhale, and lower your hands, palms facing down, as you exhale. Coordinate your movement with your breathing; if your breathing is shallow, the movement of your hands up and down will be small, and if your breathing is deep, your hands will go up and down with larger movements Repeat this breathing and movement for several minutes until you are ready to stop. When you feel ready to stop moving, sit for a moment, breathing quietly as you pay attention. You may even feel a slight tingling and vitality in your arms. Then, after a minute or two, stretch and open your eyes.

Exercise 8.11: Calming Breathing by Allowing

The next meditation will teach you how to calm your breathing. Often people think that they have to *make* themselves calm down. But the meditative way is to learn how to allow and permit breathing, then calming follows naturally.

This meditation teaches you how to permit and let be. Practice this exercise for several minutes. Increase the time to 15 minutes each, as you are able.

Sit or lie down in a comfortable position. Scan through your body with your attention, without changing anything. Simply notice what you experience. Sense your breathing. Is it easy? Labored? Slow? Quick? Notice without changing anything. In this approach, you do not try to deliberately change your breathing; rather, you allow the change to take place naturally. Can you allow your whole rib cage to take part in your breathing? Can you permit your abdomen to relax and move with your breathing? Can you feel your lower back and waist move? Can you feel your shoulders move? Let yourself breathe just as you do, without interfering or holding the breath back, while at the same time not trying to breathe more deeply or more shallowly. Wait and allow your body to respond naturally and automatically. Allow your breath to find its natural way.

CONCLUSION

When working with focus meditation in psychotherapy, invite clients to have an experience. Imagery works well with some people, who immediately feel comfortable with focusing on a picture and visualizing it within. For others, breathing is a better object of focus. Try both ways with your clients. You might be surprised to discover that what works for you might not be as helpful for a client. But what you find difficult to do may be natural for a client. If you familiarize yourself with both forms of focus meditation, you will be open to the needs and talents of your clients.

9

Open-Focus Meditation: Mindfulness

Core Principle 9: Be Mindful in the Present Moment to Attune to Thoughts, Feelings, and Behaviors.

This [mindfulness] is the direct way, monks, for the purification of beings, for the overcoming of sorrow and lamentation, for the extinguishing of suffering and grief, for walking on the path of truth, for the realization of [nirvana].

—*Buddha,* Mahasatipatthana Sutta

INTRODUCTION

One of the most widely used forms of meditation for therapy is mindfulness. The value of teaching clients how to be in touch with what they are doing, thinking, and feeling as they experience is healing in and of itself. And the skills they gain will facilitate their ability to work better in therapy and engage more fully and realistically in their life.

Mindfulness practices focus awareness on each breath, body sensation, emotion, and thought in an open, ever-changing flow of new experiences.

As an open-focus form of meditation, the object of focus changes moment by moment. Attention is combined with awareness anew in the present. Researchers have found that when people can be aware of the mind and body in the present, they tend to have more realistic and grounded responses (Grossman, Niemann, Schmidt, & Walach, 2004; Hankey, 2006). Then they can know what they experience, and, with that information, they are more likely to do what is best for them.

This chapter provides mindfulness instructions that can be added into the therapy session and performed by therapists and clients between sessions. We teach how to take a nonjudgmental attitude, without evaluation or conceptualization. We provide the classic mindfulness meditations of body, emotions, mind, and presence in the moment. This practice has benefits for both therapists and clients, not just for better regulation of affect, more centered and aware behavior, and easing of troubling thoughts and sensations, but also for deepening enjoyment of everyday life. This story illustrates how we can have great joy, even from the simple things, when we are mindful.

Well-being Here and Now

A Buddhist master lived in a simple hut far from any village. One evening the monk was out walking, mindfully aware of his surroundings. Meanwhile, a robber had entered the hut. The robber looked all around for goods to steal but could find nothing. Just then the monk came home and saw the robber. The monk said, "You have traveled a great distance to visit me. I wouldn't want you to leave with nothing. Please, let me give you the shirt I'm wearing."

The robber was puzzled by this strange offer but took the shirt and left. Then the monk sat down and meditated on the moon, whose wonderful clear light shone through his open window. "Poor robber," he thought. "If only I could give him this stunning moon!"

This story illustrates how the mindful monk's appreciation of the moon and compassion for his fellow human beings brought him a sense of peace and well-being. Many of our clients live their lives dwelling on negative people and experiences, missing the positive possibilities that are also there.

Mindfulness is an approach to life, a way of opening attention to the full range of ongoing experiencing. By introducing mindfulness to your clients, you release a vast vista of potential that deeper awareness can bring.

BRIEF HISTORY OF MINDFULNESS IN CONTEXT

Mindfulness is a practice with a long history in philosophical and religious tradition. It has developed from this context into a secular one, becoming central in the modern application of meditation to psychotherapy.

Mindfulness formally began with Theravada Buddhism, the earlier form of Buddhism, which was described by the Buddha in the *Mahasatipatthana Sutta: The Great Discourse on the Establishing of Awareness* (1996) as a special kind of insight where the meditator is simply mindful of the changing phenomena of experience. Earlier philosophical and religious traditions in Hindu thought, most notably the Vedas, encouraged attitudes, beliefs, and states of consciousness through song and poetry but didn't have a conception of attention to consciousness itself. Other cultures might have had some disciplined practices that used thought processes, but currently there is no accepted record of anything like the practice of mindfulness. For example, ancient Greek philosophy did not include consciousness in its theory during this period, although there was attention to subtle aspects of language use, conceptions, and the assumptions behind them. Certain philosophers, such as the Skeptics, did theorize about sentiments and experience, seeking *akrasia*, the comfortable suspension of thought, reached through epistemological speculation. The great Greek philosopher Aristotle was concerned about emotion, among his wide range of interests. He taught how to evoke emotions for rhetorical purposes as well as how to find and use an emotional mean (middle way) as part of leading the good life. Later, Roman thought dealt with sentiment, especially with regard to rhetoric and coming to terms with emotion using rational philosophical calm. But Buddha was the first person to point consciousness to itself. He began the tradition of conscious exploration of personal experience by means of attentive awareness that we know in modern times as mindfulness.

Buddha believed that the way to enlightenment was through one's own efforts. And he taught mindfulness as a method for reaching it. He carefully followed each moment of awareness. He believed that by staying with what he experienced and thought about, everything became an opportunity for living in enlightenment.

Today mindfulness has taken on a wider meaning. The fact that mindfulness has become a secular practice extends its usefulness tremendously, beyond its original application in a religious context.

The original practice of mindfulness was to bring about the state of mind that Buddha encouraged: fully present, fully thoughtful, deeply immersed in the moment to moment experience. The Buddha held that when conscious experience is carefully attended to, accurate clear understanding becomes possible, which then shows the path of correct action toward what is experienced. In Western thought, consciousness is consciousness of *something*. It is turned toward an object, and by the word *object*, we do not just refer to an external thing. We mean much more.

George Herbert Mead, a foundational figure in American sociology, defined an object as anything we can attend to, including inner experience and events. Through the mindful use of the mind, directed in this way to outer and inner experiences, objects of consciousness can be examined and analyzed, in order to come to a higher level of understanding. Mindful attention leads to a perspective of detachment from concerns that don't really matter. According to the great Western philosopher Martin Heidegger (1889–1976), as soon as we exist, we are inseparable from the world. We cannot exist without a world to exist in. Mindfulness gets us in touch with that world, and then we can let go of stressful conflicts and concerns. The practitioner of mindfulness begins with suspending judgment and focusing in a concentrated way. We describe many methods for doing this in this chapter.

Mindfulness is now being integrated into Western forms of meditation as a helpful therapeutic tool to center clients and practitioners in conscious experience.

MINDFULNESS RESEARCH

Thanks to the extensive mindfulness research conducted by Jon Kabat Zinn, therapists can be confident that mindfulness has scientific evidence for using it in psychotherapy. In the early years of researching mindfulness, Jon Kabat-Zinn et al. (1992) performed careful research that was to revolutionize psychotherapy. He carried out an experiment that demonstrated the effects of mindfulness on stress over an eight-week period. The group of subjects agreed to certain stringent conditions, most important of which was to meditate with mindfulness as their technique a number of times a day for eight weeks. The research was conducted to determine whether the subjects could reduce stress measurably only by practicing mindfulness. This study demonstrated that mindfulness meditation by itself is an effective way to reduce stress. Kabat-Zinn's groundbreaking project led to a great deal of confirming research, which continues today. In 2013, Kabat-Zinn published an expansion of the model from its narrow application to stress, with empirical verification of many practical therapeutic problems including anxiety, substance abuse, depression, and trauma.

Today, the practice of mindfulness includes more varied techniques, which we will be including in this chapter and in Part V. And there is another benefit to varying the technique of mindfulness. Using a variety of techniques provides a larger context of experiences to learn from and can be adapted to the unique needs of each client.

Mindfulness is more than any one specific practice can encompass. Mindfulness becomes the state of being mindful, evolving from a process of awareness. Researchers found that as people meditate over time, a change takes place. Mindfulness affects the brain differently depending on whether the meditator is a novice or has been doing it for a long time. Research shows that the brain takes on new patterns that foster awareness and self regulation, which they call "dispositional mindfulness." Seasoned meditators activate an extensive network of brain areas that allow the emotions to be noticed and regulated. The network involves increased links between the attention areas of the cortex and the limbic system (Brown, Goodman, & Inzlicht, 2013).

After dispositional mindfulness is elicited, it is easier to maintain. There is a certain momentum. And as the state of dispositional mindfulness becomes stable, a shift occurs, toward calmer reactions and better self-regulation in general, even if you are not meditating. So, as you concentrate attention through the specific practices, you elicit a more generalized reaction. The specific practice leads you to the state of being mindful in your life. When you feel ready, permit the state to take place, to emerge for you. Then mindfulness becomes an experience itself, a change of state. It is as if you open a door with the specific practice and then walk through it to the mindful space. Be exacting at first, in order to train well. Then you make your mindful awareness automatic; it will take less effort and flow naturally.

The usual way of performing mindfulness is in the present moment. The exercises emphasize this, in respect to its origins and adaptation to the foundational model. But as mindfulness has evolved, it has grown to incorporate much more, with flexible boundaries. And time is one of those boundaries. Mindfulness can be extended into time, to help anticipate and project awareness forward or backward.

MINDFULNESS OVERVIEW

Although mindfulness requires attention in order to initiate, mindfulness is different from our typical ways of paying attention.

Typically we notice something and then we have thoughts about it. We make judgments, liking or disliking what we are experiencing. Or we might assess it, decided whether it's something good or, perhaps, bad. At other times, an experience reminds of something from the past, which leads us to compare it to that previous experience. Or we might expect the experience to influence a later event, imagining a future that is altered.

Mindfulness involves setting all of this cognitive activity aside and instead staying with just the experience itself as it occurs in the present. It can be understood as having three components: 1) Staying in the present moment, 2) Being nonjudgmental, and 3) Accepting each experience just as it is. When mindfulness is engaged in, attention opens the door to a new experience. But the inner essence remains: Mind.

There are many ways to vary mindfulness, and later exercises in this chapter offer some possibilities. There are also many possible applications, whether mindfulness is applied to such things as parenting and social interactions or to internal concerns, such as emotional regulation. Later chapters provide therapeutic applications you can use.

Below you will find an exercise to practice each of the three components, and then bring it altogether in mindful practice.

Exercise 9.1: Staying in the Present Moment

In general, mindfulness is the act of paying close attention to each experience, moment to moment, letting go of the moment before, embracing the present moment, without concern for anticipating the moment to come. Eventually, a change in the state of consciousness takes place, and the moment itself is experienced differently.

This may not be easy at first. We all tend to want to make assessments, and there is an appropriate time for this. But during this exercise, simply attend to the present experience, and allow it to fill your mind. Let go of the past experience: It is no more. Suspend your concern for the future. It is not yet. Stay with the present experiencing. This is what is, for now. Then allow the next moment to emerge, attending fully to each new moment as it comes. This is the essence of the practice of mindfulness.

Exercise 9.2: Developing the Nonjudgmental Attitude

A nonjudgmental attitude is essential to the practice of mindfulness. Such an attitude means suspending judgment while remaining centered in awareness, moment to moment. Typically, we think of things, react to our thoughts and feelings about them, associate and categorize, putting our thoughts in perspective. Each of us has our personal view, naturally, and assessment helps us to know ourselves in the world. But during this exercise, our personal view should not be the focus of attention. Don't judge or assess the experience. Instead suspend judgment and notice each experience, without evaluation or consideration of the merit or lack of merit in what is in awareness: the content.

But not judging does not mean encouraging the lack of correct judgment. Mindfulness engages thought in a different manner than evaluative thinking. Think of mindful awareness like a scientist running an experiment. She begins by observing the data. She can't decide what the data means, whether it's good or bad, until all the facts have been collected. Judgment would be premature. Because the judgment of good or bad often requires comparison to an external standard, the judging process takes you away from the experience itself. This is antithetical to the intent of mindfulness. Mindfulness is directed to the flow of consciousness. By staying mindfully present with each moment, you gain a fuller, clearer awareness of what is actually occurring in consciousness, here and now.

We have had clients, especially those with impulse control problems or criminality, say, "Does this mean I can do whatever I want?" We clarify that behavior, of course, must always abide by the laws of the land. We are not free to do anything we want because we live in a society with others. Non-judgmental awareness of mindfulness concerns the flow of consciousness. Mindfulness is non-judgmental of our experiencing.

Begin by paying attention to your body sensations. Simply notice the qualities of your sensations. Set aside any judgment for now, even if a sensation is uncomfortable. Simply notice it just as it is. Can you discern the qualities of your sensory experiences: Soft, hard, warm, cool, calm, tight, soft, etc. Resist the impulse to assess. Take a neutral stance instead and simply be aware of the flow of your consciousness around your sensations as they unfold, moment-by-moment. Notice how they change as you move through time. And if you notice yourself judging, don't judge the judgment. Simply notice, "Now I am judging," and move on to noticing sensations just as they are.

Exercise 9.3: Fostering Mindfulness by Accepting Yourself from Head to Toe

Accepting each experience is an important aspect of mindful awareness, but people often misunderstand what acceptance really means. We have had clients ask us, "Are you saying that I should give up and not try to change?" Our answer is "No!" Typically, when people have an uncomfortable feeling or experience, they try to get away from it. But in avoiding, they lose the opportunity to truly understand the feeling or experience more fully. This is what psychotherapy is all about, helping people to get in touch with their conflicts so that they can discover solutions. As you accept each experience just as it is, even the uncomfortable ones, you are in the best position to know that experience deeply. And in knowing that experience and staying with it as it unfolds through time, you undergo transformation.

Learn to accept your experience of yourself without making comparisons or criticisms. Then you will be able to appreciate your qualities just as they are. As you practice refraining from judgment you will notice details of your experience, your actions, and their effects that you probably didn't perceive before. Some of the Buddhist sutras encouraged people to focus attention on all the negative impurities and unattractive physical aspects of themselves and their world. The aim was for the practitioner to train the mind to accept the bad along with the good, to dismiss concern with trivial matters, and cultivate acceptance of things just as they are. So, try to become aware of what is there, and accept whatever you notice, good or bad, pleasant or unpleasant. Keep your observations clear and descriptive.

To foster self-acceptance, survey yourself from head to toe and recognize all your different parts. Typically, we like some things about ourselves and dislike others, such as I like my hair, but my nose is too big. Traditionally, Buddhism counted 32 body parts. Describe each part to yourself. Notice, for example, your hair, its color, texture, and style; your eyes; and other attributes. But stay factual and accept each part, just as it is. For example, observe that your hair is long, dark brown, and curly. But don't add an evaluation, such as attractive or unattractive.

This exercise might be easy to do if you are a model or movie star, with a perfect body and minimal faults, but most of us have what we consider to be flaws. Mindfulness can help you to accept yourself, even if you believe that you have serious deficiencies. Embrace what you notice now about your body without belittling yourself or complimenting yourself. Observe and notice what is there, but don't pass judgment and sincerely accept each part, just as it is.

Exercise 9.4: Accepting Something Neutral, Unpleasant, and Pleasant

Sit comfortably in a chair, and let your eyes gently close if you would like. Then breathe for a moment until you find a relaxed rhythm. Now turn your attention to a neutral sensation, perhaps the feeling of your feet touching the floor. Notice it and accept it just as it is, slight pressure on the bottoms of your feet, or warmth, or whatever you feel.

Next, let your attention flow to an uncomfortable feeling in your body. Perhaps you have a slight tightness in a neck muscle, or maybe you are feeling hungry. Notice this sensation and its qualities: Is it a pressure feeling or a tightness? Or perhaps you feel a burning or rumbling? Be curious to discover as many qualities as you can, and accept each one, noticing just what it is as you notice it.

Finally, turn your attention to a pleasant experience in your body. Perhaps your breathing feels relaxing, or maybe it's a pleasant temperature of your skin. Whatever it is, once again, notice the qualities of this experience—perhaps softness, or gentle movement, or lightness or heaviness, warmth or coolness. Once again, accept each quality just as it is.

Now just sit and accept each moment's experience as it occurs, noticing what it is and accepting it as it is. Then when you are ready, stand up and stretch. You may find that in accepting the full range of your experiencing in this way, you are attuned and at ease.

PRACTICING MINDFULNESS OF BODY, EMOTIONS, AND THOUGHTS

This series of exercises can open the path to this moment-by-moment awareness by beginning with focusing on the body, followed by emotions, and then thoughts. Finally, we bring it all together in the present moment, without judgment, accepting each experience just as it is.

Mindfulness of Your Body

You can initiate mindfulness by turning attention to something readily available: noticing your body.

Exercise 9.5: Noticing Body Positions

Warm up with a generalized sense of body awareness. Start by noticing your body position and movements at times while sitting, standing, lying down, and walking. When you are going about your day, take a moment to notice your body sensations in each of these positions. We often pay very little attention to such fundamentals, yet our body sensations, or their absence, are an inseparable part of all the body positions we take in life, an important and valuable experience to tune in to. So, when you first wake up in the morning, begin by taking a moment to notice yourself lying in bed. Then as you get up, pay attention to how you sit up, step onto the floor, and slowly stand up. Notice the details of your body position as you walk to the bathroom, as you wash your face, and brush your teeth. Take note of your body positioning and allow yourself to sense each position carefully whenever you have a chance throughout your day.

Exercise 9.6: Mindfulness of Body: Exploring a Body Position

Delve a little deeper and pay attention to one particular body position. For example, when sitting on a chair somewhere in your house, notice your posture.

Are you sitting straight, leaning, or slumping into the chair? Do you take support from the chair or push down on the seat? Are certain muscles tight while others are looser? Where are your feet and your hands? Is your neck straining or relaxed? Pay close attention to these and other details as you sit now in this chair.

Exercise 9.7: Following Mindfulness of Body

Now sit quietly and turn your attention to your body. You might notice how your feet meet the floor. Perhaps next your attention is drawn to your back as it meets the chair. Follow the flow of your awareness wherever it freely goes, but keep it on your body experience. Stay with your body sensations and experiences without judging them good or bad or something you like or dislike. Simply notice your experience fully and attentively with each passing moment. You might perceive that your body experience changes as you observe. Perhaps you noticed tightness somewhere and found yourself letting it go. Stay attuned over time, open to what the next moment brings. Doing this permits the flowing awareness of mindfulness of the body.

Mindfulness of Feelings

Emotions are an important component of living, and so mindfulness must include attention to feelings. Mindfulness has a clear method for dealing with emotions in a way that can overcome suffering and maximize fulfillment.

Feelings can be categorized as pleasant, unpleasant, or neutral. People tend to cling to pleasant feelings and reject unpleasant ones. But this clinging and rejecting sets in motion a secondary set of reactions that interferes with awareness and causes suffering. You will be able to drop the secondary reaction as you become more aware of and accept the feelings themselves, just as they are. Acceptance in this way leads to more comfortable reactions.

Exercise 9.8: Accepting Emotions

Sit down for a moment and close your eyes. Turn your attention inward, and notice what you are feeling right now. Perhaps you feel calm, or perhaps a little tense as you sit without moving. Notice the feeling, whatever it is. Then pay attention to how the feeling begins to alter a bit as you notice it. Perhaps the accompanying sensations increase or decrease. Or maybe another feeling emerges. Stay with the flow of your emotions as time passes, and remember to set aside any typical judgments you may have about such feelings. Simply get to know each moment's experience as it is being felt now, before you articulate its meaning. Then try to put a name to your emotion or mood, matching the description with what you feel. If it is not quite right, modify your description until you feel satisfied.

If you find that you are compelled to keep making judgments, acknowledge this and say inwardly, "Now I am aware of feeling compelled to make a judgment." Be like a benevolent kindergarten teacher who watches over her students as they play on the playground. When two children begin fighting, the teacher does not become angry with them. Instead, she calmly tries to attend to their needs. Benevolently observe, in this sense of watching over, all your different feelings, even the ones you typically experience as unpleasant. By eliminating the secondary aversion reaction to a negative feeling, you will significantly lessen your suffering. The method to use is calm neutrality of attitude.

Mindfulness of Thinking

Mindfulness of thinking begins by first recognizing what you are thinking while you think it, a sort of dual action of your awareness.

Exercise 9.9: Mindfulness of What You Are Thinking

Sit quietly and close your eyes. Notice what you are thinking as you think it. Follow the flow of your thoughts. Be like someone sitting on the bank of a river who watches leaves and twigs flow down the river. Don't jump into the river but stay back on shore, observing. Keep observing and letting each thought drift past. As soon as you notice yourself being taken downstream with a thought, climb back on shore and resume your observing.

Exercise 9.10: Mindfulness of the Qualities of Thought

Next try to understand how your thinking works. We do not usually experience the world directly. Rather we experience everything through our consciousness of it.

Mindfully observe your thoughts again. Think about this statement from a Buddhist sutra: "A thought is like lightning, it breaks up in a moment and does not stay on" (Conze, 1995, p. 163). You will see the fleeting nature of thoughts as they come and go. Stay with each moment of experiencing, and you will notice how every thought lacks staying power. Even if the content of your present thought resembles earlier thoughts, each actual momentary thought is brief and then gone as a new thought arises.

Exercise 9.11: Meditating on Your Thought Process

Now turn your attention to the qualities of thinking.

Sit quietly and observe, beyond the content of what you are thinking about, the thought itself. Do your thoughts emerge in your mind quickly, or do they arise slowly? Is there a constant stream, or do you observe spaces between with little or no thought? Stay with this experience for a little while, simply noticing the qualities of your thought process itself. The qualities of thinking might alter when you observe them. Your awareness of thoughts becomes part of the thought process.

BRINGING IT ALL TOGETHER

Fritz Perls, the founder of Gestalt therapy, stated in 1969 that awareness is curative. Mindfulness research has given these wise words a scientific backing. You may be pleasantly surprised to discover how practicing mindfulness throughout the day can lead to a generalized feeling of well-being.

Exercise 9.12: Mindfulness in the Moment

Now that you have experimented with various ways of being mindful, bring yourself to the present moment. Scan your body to focus your awareness. To become mindful of your emotions, observe what you are feeling what you are thinking. How do you experience your experience of body, mind, and emotions? And then pay close attention to the objects of your perception. These four qualities of mindfulness can be done quickly, centering you in the present. Finally, once you are in touch with the moment's experiencing, let all this go and just be present, without thinking about it, just being.

CONCLUSION

Notice how your experience transforms moment by moment. Stay with each moment anew. Whenever you can, at various times during the day, turn your attention to your experience. Get in touch, mindfully, as often as you can. In time, mindfulness will feel natural. You will feel in balance with yourself and your surroundings, accepting the flow of life as it comes and acting in harmony with what is needed.

10

No-Focus Meditation: Emptiness and Letting Be

Core Principle 10: Clear Your Mind. Invite the Natural Free Flow of Potential to Emerge.

When your spirit is not in the least clouded, when the clouds of bewilderment clear away, there is the true void.
—Miyamoto Musashi, The Book of Five Rings

INTRODUCTION

Most people are accustomed to filling their time. You can observe that your clients' actions are often intentional and goal directed. And as they fill their time, so the mind often becomes filled more than they might like. You can guide them to develop a state of absorption that is formless, to let go of directing the mind deliberately, and to clear the mind of all thought. Attention is not selectively focused on anything, and, as a result, the continual flow of thoughts slows. Known in Zen Buddhism as no-mind, this quality of mind is goalless, nonconceptual, without any object of focus at all, a special kind of no focus. But it is not simply a nothing state. Many of the ancient meditation traditions call this state of no-state enlightenment.

NEUROSCIENCE OF NO FOCUS: THE DEFAULT MODE NETWORK AND UNCONSCIOUS PROBLEM SOLVING

Modern neuroscience has found that even when we are being engaged in executive functions, doing things in the world, our brain is in a network of interactions known as the task mode network (TMN). The TMN engages the executive functions in the anterior (front) part of the frontal lobes. Much of our time is engaged in this way, busy planning, organizing, and doing things.

But when we are sitting quietly, perhaps relaxing for a moment without anything in mind, the brain is still active, but in a different way. This free flow of thought without any particular direction or purpose is known in neuroscience as the default mode network (DMN). The DMN connects the medial (middle) parts of the frontal, parietal, and temporal lobes. This network is known as the resting state of the brain. We can return to the DMN at times to renew and refresh.

Although much has been gained from the deliberate use of executive functions, history shows that many of the world's great problems have been solved when the mind is set free. This true story illustrates how Otto Loewi was only able to access his insight about the presence of neurotransmitters when he was a dreaming and not in the waking state.

How One of the World's Great Discoveries Occurred as a Dream

Otto Loewi (1873–1961) had a strong belief that chemical reactions were involved in synaptic communications, but he couldn't think of any way to prove it. At this time, most people believed that the signals at the synapses between neurons were strictly electrical.

On Easter weekend in 1921, Loewi dreamed of an experiment about this problem. He awoke very excited and quickly scribbled down the idea. Then he went back to sleep, expecting to work on the problem further in the morning. But when he woke up and tried to read his notes, he was unable to decipher his handwriting. He spent what he called the worst day of his life trying to remember the experiment. But much as he tried, he couldn't bring the experiment into his conscious thought. That night he fell asleep feeling discouraged and frustrated. But as he finally drifted into a deep sleep, he had the same dream again. Thankful for a second chance, he woke up in the middle of the night delighted, and immediately went to his laboratory. The experiment he performed that night would forever change the world of neuroscience. His conscious mind could not solve his problem, but his unconscious dream gave him his solution. Loewi would earn a Nobel Prize in 1936 for this famous experiment that gave scientific evidence to the idea that the signals at the synapses were not just electrical but also involved the flow of neurotransmitters, a chemical communication.

FREE FLOW OF THE UNCONSCIOUS MIND

No-focus meditations reach into the recesses of the unconscious by letting go of the way we typically focus our attention in daily life. By not focusing on anything in particular, unconscious processes can be expressed. For example, you probably have had times when you were deeply involved in a conversation on the telephone. After you hung up, you noticed that you created many doodles unconsciously while you were talking. This free flowing of hand movement occurred out of awareness, spontaneously, without any censorship or limitations from your conscious mind. In a similar way, the next exercises help develop this natural capacity through meditation. You can imagine how helpful this can be for therapy, where we are trying to help clients free their unconscious from conflict and allow their healthy, natural spontaneous nature to emerge.

The skills that are developed in this type of no-focus meditation are often so subtle that people do not notice them at first. The experience may be very slight, but by your keeping an open and encouraging attitude, along with your client's practice and training, eventually everyone will be pleasantly surprised.

Exercise 10.1: Begin with Quiet Sitting

How turbid, like muddy water!

What may allay the muddiness?

Through stillness it will gradually become clear.

—Tao Te Ching, *translated by J. J. L. Duyvendak*

No-focus meditation begins by inviting a quiet moment. Neuroscience calls it activating the DMN. Confucianism calls it quiet sitting. How often do we give ourselves the luxury of doing nothing? Here is a free moment to let yourself be, as you simply engage in quiet sitting.

To perform this form of meditation, simply sit quietly with nothing in mind. Pick a time when you don't have any particular responsibilities. Find a comfortable sitting position. You may want to set a timer on your watch so that you can be assured to stop when you need to. Then let your mind wander. Don't think about anything in particular. Just sit quietly, without a goal or a plan. As you allow yourself just to sit quietly, you elicit the DMN, that simple resting state of mind and brain.

Exercise 10.2: Letting Your Mind Wander

Mind wandering is a way to solve problems unconsciously. By activating the DMN within the context of a problem you are working on consciously, you can activate the executive functions to tap into your creativity. We have used this technique with clients to encourage them to make their own discoveries. By being encouraging and open-ended, you provide a setting where new possibilities can emerge.

Sit quietly, as you did in the quiet sitting exercise, but with the intent of considering a problem you are working on. Then, without thinking about the problem, invite yourself to daydream. Let your thoughts drift and mind wander where it will. Don't deliberately think about anything; simply let your mind go, to drift and dream. You might have an image or perhaps a significant memory. The connections might not make sense. But you may be surprised to find, either now or later, that your daydream leads you to a new solution.

Exercise 10.3: Inviting the Flow: Attention to Your Hands

Sit in a chair, with both your feet flat on the floor. Let your hands rest on your legs, palms down. Close your eyes. Direct your attention to your hands. Applying the same open-ended approach as in the previous exercise, wonder what you might experience in your hands. Will they feel light or heavy? Warm or cool? Perhaps you might notice a tingling in your fingertips. Ask yourself whether one hand feels lighter or heavier, warmer or cooler, or more tingly than the other. Allow any differences to occur, and observe carefully. Enjoy the experience. When you are ready, return to scanning outwardly. Open your eyes and stretch.

Exercise 10.4: Free Flow of Attention Exercise

Sit in a comfortable chair and lean back, relaxed. Close your eyes and allow your body to relax. Let your thoughts drift. Do not think about anything in particular. Relax your breathing, but do not direct your breaths in any particular way. You do not need to think of anything or do anything in particular. Simply wait, open-minded, wondering what your unconscious mind would like to present. Sometimes people feel as if they are floating, sometimes sinking. You might experience a warmth or coolness, or perhaps an image will come to mind. Do not try to have any particular experience, simply allow what is. When you are finished, open your eyes and stretch.

CLEARING THE MIND

Clearing the mind of all thought is another no-focus meditation practice. How can you go to the default mode, to clear your mind of thoughts at will, to be formlessly absorbed when so many thoughts are passing through your mind? The answer is somewhat counterintuitive, as this story illustrates. Mind clearing is not what you might think, as this legendary story from the annals of Zen history illustrates.

Discovering the Clear Mind Within

Bodhidharma is considered the founder of Zen Buddhism, but Hui-neng (638–713), the Sixth Patriarch, brought about a new way to clear the mind and find enlightenment. Unlike all the previous patriarchs who were highly educated, Hui-neng was a poor, illiterate firewood cutter. One day, just after selling some firewood in the market, he overheard a man reciting one of the most famous Buddhist

(continued)

(*continued*)

sutras, the Diamond Sutra (Jewel of Transcendental Wisdom). Unexpectedly, and in a flash of sudden insight, Hui-neng was enlightened.

Following this profound transformation, Hui-neng wanted to deepen his insight. He journeyed to the famous temple of Hung-jen, the Fifth Patriarch of Zen, and asked him to accept him as a student. In those days, monasteries usually did not allow uneducated people to join, but Hung-jen recognized that this seeker had natural talent. And so, even though Hui-neng was just a simple worker, he was accepted as a lay monk and given the job of pounding rice and splitting firewood.

Time passed, and Hung-jen was ready to retire and appoint a successor. He decided to hold a contest to determine the successor. He asked all his students to compose a poem that epitomized their insight. Shen-hsui, the senior student, was naturally expected to be given the official robe and bowl signifying direct transmission. Shen-hsui's poem read:

> Our body is the bodhi tree
> And our mind a mirror bright
> Carefully we wipe them hour-by-hour
> And let no dust alight.
>
> —Price and Mou-lam (1990, p. 70)

On hearing this poem, Hui-neng felt that he had a deeper insight and composed his own poem:

> There is no bodhi tree
> Nor stand of a mirror bright
> Since all is void,
> Where can the dust alight?
>
> —Price and Mou-lam (1990, p. 72)

The master listened to both poems and recognized Hui-neng's wisdom. He decided to recognize Shen-Hsiu for his years of devoted service and study but awarded Hui-neng the honor of starting his own school of Zen in the South. Hui-neng's school flourished, becoming the dominant tradition, and most Zen schools today trace their roots to Hui-neng. Based on his own experience, Hui-neng firmly believed that "the essence of mind is already pure and free" (Price & Mou-lam, 1990, p. 73). Neither long study nor unusual talent was necessary to have a clear mind. Once this simple truth is realized, anyone from a lowly peasant to a royal king could have this transformative experience.

You can't bring about a clear mind by trying simply to wipe away all your thoughts like polishing the dust off a mirror. Instead, in the meditative moment, you flow naturally with your deeper spiritual nature and discover a calm, clear mind. This form of meditation taps into the unconscious and brings an experience of self-transformation.

Instructions are given below for emptiness meditations, which lead to a quieting of the mental chatter naturally and effortlessly.

Exercise 10.5: From Free Flow to Still Mind

Letting-be meditations teach how to let go and follow the natural flow. The key is to align yourself with the natural forces, like a bird riding the wind. Developing the ability to allow your attention to be flexible and free is an important skill for quieting your mind. This meditation brings your mind to stillness without trying to do so.

Notice a time with no immediate responsibilities or obligations coupled with less spontaneous mental activity. Look for such a moment, perhaps at night, just before sleep, during a lunch break, or a time alone with nothing that has to be done. Another possibility is to find a time when attention wants to drift or the mind feels blank. In moments like these, you could try to force yourself to do a chore or task. But instead, use such a moment as an opportunity to develop open attention.

Spend a few minutes permitting your mind to be blank, and explore how expansive that blankness can be. Do not try to discern what it is exactly, but allow this spontaneous tendency for your consciousness to drift for a few minutes.

This state of mind may happen sitting, standing, or even when waiting in line for a long time. The important thing is to notice the moment of opportunity and allow the experience to take place when circumstances permit. Let your thoughts drift. Don't do anything and don't think about anything in particular. Simply be quiet, allowing this experience to develop. After you have experienced a naturally occurring brief moment of blankness, you may find that you can deliberately access this open attention.

Exercise 10. 6: Allowing Thoughts to Settle with an Image

Imagine that you are sitting on the shore of a pond. The pond is alive with activity. Frogs croak; crickets sing; birds fly overhead; a fish jumps out of the water, feeding on insects, splashes back, and jumps again after a bit, in another spot. Wind whips over the water, stirring up the muddy bottom. All is movement. Then gradually, as the day passes, the conditions begin to shift. The wind dies down. The frogs settle in for a nap, the crickets are silent, the birds perch in the trees, the fish stops jumping and waits. The pond is quiet. The murky rippled surface calms as the mud sinks to the bottom, and the water is again crystal clear, reflecting the natural surroundings. All is stillness. Imagine this scene vividly. Stay with the quiet, crystal-clear water.

Exercise 10.7: Mirror Mind Meditation

When the perfect man employs his mind, it is a mirror. It conducts nothing and anticipates nothing. Thus, he is able to deal successfully with all things, and injures none.
—Taoist Sage Chuang-Tzu in The Writings of Chuang Tzu, *in James Legge*

Here is a metaphor that may help you to clear your mind, imagining for a moment that your mind is a mirror. You can keep returning to the clear mirror, empty yet reflecting everything else, and, through that image, discover your clear, empty mind.

Sit upright on the floor, legs crossed, hands resting on your lap. Close your eyes. Vividly visualize your mind as a mirror, clear and empty. All that you see in the mirror is just a reflection of the world, both outer and inner. Keep this image of a mirror reflecting nothing. If a thought occurs to you, see it as a reflection in the mirror, knowing it is not the mirror, only the reflection. Let the mirror of your mind clear again. Eventually fewer reflections will appear, until your mirror mind remains clear.

Exercise 10.8: Classic Zen Meditation

Zen, sitting meditation, is the classic exercise used in Zen Buddhism. Zen monks spend many hours meditating in this way, seeking to bring about an enlightened state of consciousness that continues to develop as they practice. Follow the instructions carefully, and with time and practice, you will experience a special calm and quiet awareness that comes from somewhere unknown, within you.

Sit upright, cross-legged, with your hands palms up and the backs resting on your thighs. Let your body be upright and straight—but not rigid—without leaning either left or right. Your head should be held straight with your ears and shoulders parallel to each other. Hold your tongue loosely against your palate and keep your lips closed and teeth together. Eyes should be closed or half open.

Breathe calmly and regularly. As you begin to meditate, clear your mind of all thought. When a thought does arise, notice it and then let it go, returning to your calm, clear mind. By continuing to do this over time, eventually you will find that thoughts intrude less and less and that your concentration becomes natural and profound.

CONCLUSION

The everyday mind can fill like a muddy pond, stirred up by thoughts, plans, and worries. Many forms of meditation use emptiness as the pathway to reduce distractions. Beyond words, clear mind is a limitless perspective, the meditative perspective. This quality of absorption opens the way for inner work. By experimenting with these exercises, your clients will discover a new-found sense of themselves, centered in their intuition.

PART V

APPLICATIONS

11

Cultivating Happiness through Compassion and Gratitude

Core Principle 11: Nurture Happiness by Practicing Compassion and Gratitude.

Gratitude is not only the greatest of all virtues, but the parent of all others.
—Cicero (106–43 BC)

INTRODUCTION

Long ago, Socrates asked the question: Can virtue be taught? New research on gratitude indicates that the answer to Socrates's question is *yes*. There is an ever-growing body of research on compassion and gratitude, with evidence for their health-promoting value. Studies have looked at the general effects of gratitude and compassion on psychological problems. One study (Kendler et al., 2003) found that the presence of gratitude as thankfulness predicted lower levels of major depression, generalized anxiety disorder, phobias, and various substance abuse problems, including alcohol dependence, drug abuse, and nicotine dependence. People can develop this virtuous quality through meditative practices.

When people embrace feeling compassion and gratitude, they experience more well-being. Even clients who have made poor choices or who suffer from years of emotional disturbance can change the courses of their lives by these practices. Because research shows the psychological benefits of compassion and gratitude, you can feel confident in adding meditations on compassion and gratitude to your therapeutic work. This chapter teaches gratitude meditations that will help your clients transform their negative adjustment into positive, fulfilling lives. And we have included other guided compassion and gratitude meditations in the application chapters in this part of the book.

NEUROSCIENCE ON GRATITUDE AND COMPASSION

You may not realize that people are wired to be happy. The nervous system has a built-in mechanism for pleasure and reward. When clients come to us feeling unhappy, their nervous system is out of balance. The reward pathway of the brain manufactures and releases the neurotransmitter dopamine, which is associated with feelings of pleasure and reward (see Figure 11.1).

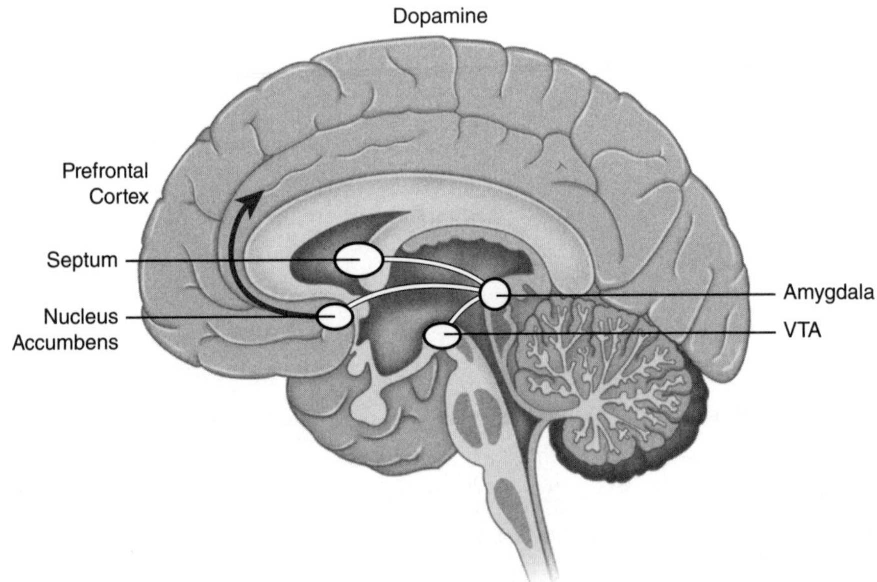

Figure 11.1   Reward Pathway

The activities we find rewarding, such as eating, sleeping, drinking, and sex, make evolutionary sense for perpetuating the species. We feel enjoyment when engaged in these activities, which classical learning theory predicts results in these activities being reinforced. The hypothalamus helps to regulate the reward system so that we maintain a healthy cycle for hunger, thirst, and sleep.

Substance abusers suffer from a compromised reward pathway, where the substance becomes wired into the pathway. Anyone who has treated clients who suffer from addiction knows that such clients get all of their satisfactions from the substance to which they are addicted and lose their enjoyment of life's natural pleasures.

In problems such as anxiety and trauma, the nervous system is on high alert, responding to feelings of danger and threat. The hypothalamus-pituitary-adrenal (HPA) pathway is activated, which streamlines many of the normal functions to prepare the body for the fight or flight reaction (see Figure 11.2). Normal sleep, eating, and drinking are disrupted, so people often feel a loss of appetite or thirst or too much eating and drinking along with difficulty sleeping.

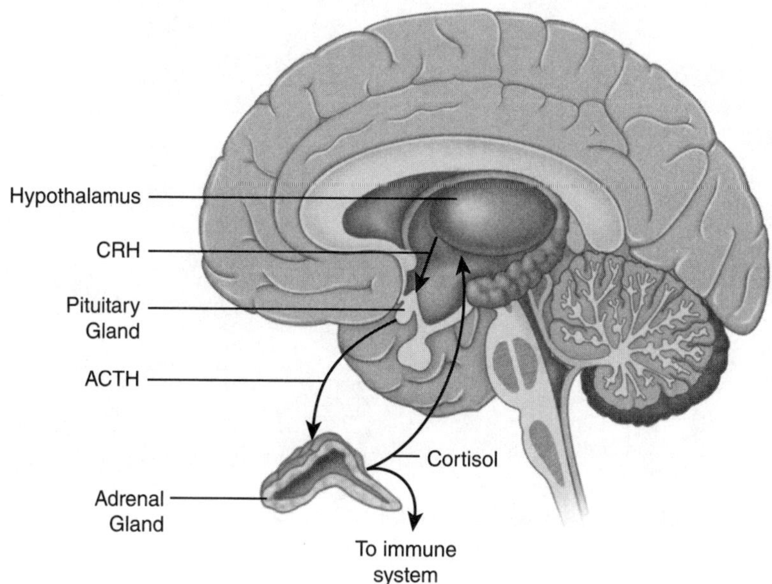

Figure 11.2   HPA Pathway

In depression, the HPA pathway signals threat, but according to Seligman's learned helplessness theory (Seligman, Steen, Park, & Peterson, 2005), the response is not to respond, which explains how depressed people are lethargic, unmotivated, and inactive. Posttraumatic stress disorder (PTSD) alters the brain: There is overactivation in the amygdala and lower activation in the anterior cingulate cortex, prefrontal cortex, thalamus, hippocampus, and occipital lobes (See Figure 11.3). These deactivations are correlated with learned helplessness, which many depressed people experience (LoLordo & Overmier, 2011). Thus, clients with this disorder do not handle emotion well, and they are ruminating without regulating.

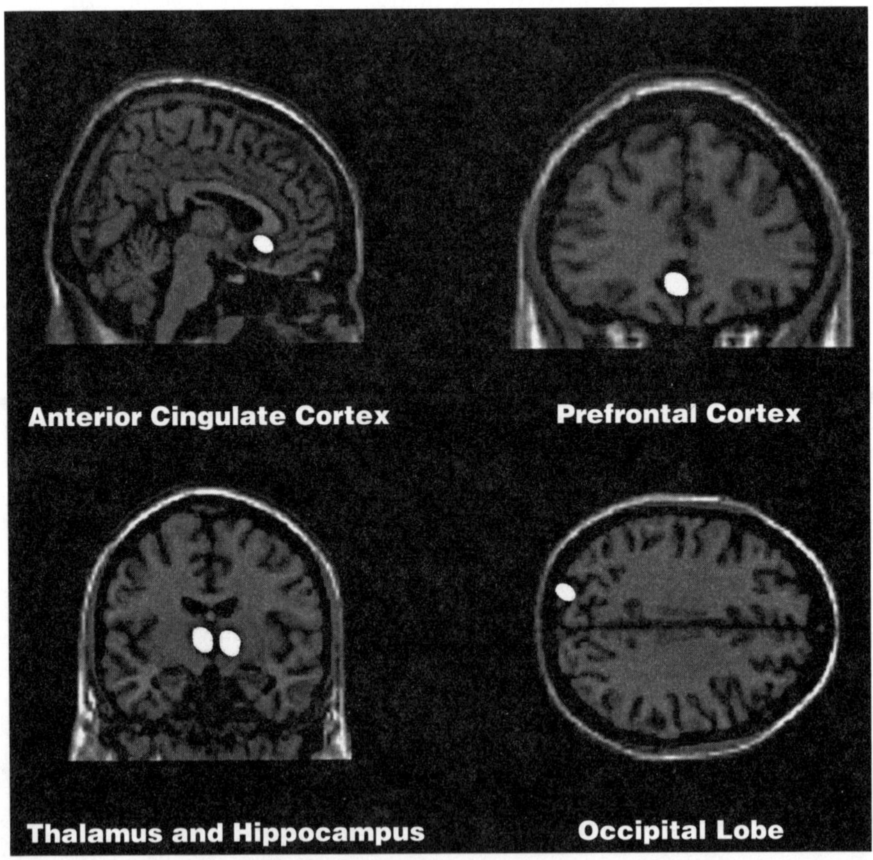

Figure 11.3   Deactivations from PTSD

How Gratitude and Compassion Change the Brain

Gratitude and compassion practice increases the brain areas involved in the production and release of dopamine. This increase in dopamine helps to explain why people feel good when practicing gratitude meditations. In addition, gratitude practice increases blood flow to the hypothalamus, the regulator of the stress response. The hypothalamus also plays a large role in the regulation of many vital body functions. Increases in the hypothalamus help to normalize the vital body functions. People begin to find it easier to sleep and maintain regular eating and drinking habits. Through these brain area changes, gratitude and compassion practice helps to lower the stress response, lessen depression, lower anxiety, and decrease minor aches and pains (Zahn et al., 2009).

Other studies have begun to show another way that gratitude and compassion may be helping to enhance how stress is coped with. Findings in affective neuroscience provide evidence, based in neuroplasticity, that developing feelings of gratitude may contribute positively to growth in neural architecture that supports better affect regulation. People who suffer from depression, anxiety, and schizophrenia have smaller volumes of limbic system connectivity, leading to deficits in the ability to regulate their emotional reactions. Development of gratitude will help in countering these affect system deficits (Garland et al., 2010; Simpkins & Simpkins, 2011).

THERAPEUTIC RATIONALES FOR INCLUDING GRATITUDE IN THERAPY

Therapy can and *should* nurture positive feelings in addition to helping people to overcome their conflicts and problems. In fact, research shows that creating an upward spiral of positive emotions tends to counter the downward spiral of negativity (Garland et al., 2010). Positive and negative emotions are two sides of the same dynamic whole (Tao) that makes us the passionate creatures we are, capable of a wide range of emotions. Sometimes, by addressing the positive in our clients, we make it easier for them to overcome the negative. Thus, an important component of good therapy is to help clients cultivate positive emotions that lead to a healthier lifestyle.

Regular practice of meditation provides techniques to activate the natural capacity for happiness and well-being. Many different research groups (e.g., Alexander, Rainforth, & Gelderloos, 1991; Brown & Ryan, 2003; Wallace & Shapiro, 2006) have found that meditators feel at ease in the world and with others. They express compassion and love toward others and toward themselves. And they tend to have feelings of well-being.

Gratitude and compassion practice has been identified as an effective intervention by the Positive Psychology movement (Seligman, Steen, Park, & Peterson, 2005). A British research team (Wood, Froh, & Geraghty, 2010) did an extensive study of gratitude and well-being, offering a compelling argument for why adding gratitude practice into psychotherapy is valuable. They point out correlations between the practice of simple gratitude exercises (like the ones in this chapter) and feeling positive emotions and well-being.

Gratitude practice can be introduced with techniques that are easy for clients to do. Three types of gratitude techniques have been carefully researched: (1) daily listing of things one is grateful for, (2) contemplating gratitude, and (3) performing behaviors that express gratitude. These and other exercises are included later in this chapter.

Gratitude and Compassion as a Possible Nonspecific Factor of Therapy

Decades of psychotherapy research have found that certain nonspecific factors play a key role in effective psychotherapy. Early psychotherapy effectiveness findings, initiated by the Johns Hopkins Phipps Clinic Research team in the 1950s and followed over 25 years (Reported in Frank, Hoehn-Saric, Imber, Liberman, & Stone, 1978), found that the presence of hope, faith, trust, positive expectancy, and a strong therapeutic relationship were some of the important predictors of therapeutic success (Frank & Frank, 1991). These findings continue to stand the test of time (Hubble, Duncan, & Miller, 2000).

Gratitude and compassion practice can be classified as a nonspecific factor for effective psychotherapy. Research has found evidence that the presence of gratitude and compassion fosters a general sense of well-being and is correlated with better mental health. The research cited shows how gratitude is linked with improved quality of life and enhanced sense of well-being in general. All forms of therapy can benefit from adding this nonspecific factor to treatments.

GRATITUDE AND COMPASSION PRACTICES

Gratitude can be cultivated by deliberate practices. These exercises offer a number of different ways to nurture gratitude in your clients. We also give some exercises for working with gratitude therapeutically.

Exercise 11.1: Grateful in Nature

An easy way to initiate gratitude is to appreciate nature. The famous philosopher Immanuel Kant believed that all human beings share a feeling of awe when viewing a beautiful sunset. We all have a natural tendency to appreciate nature, and this may be a good place to start with some clients who have difficulty feeling positive emotions.

Go somewhere outdoors in nature—a local park, your own backyard, a beach, or a grassy area under a tree. You can also start the exercise in your office by bringing in a beautiful plant or bouquet of flowers. Sit down and let your thoughts settle. Listen to the sounds, feel the breeze, notice the temperature. Pay attention to the air as you breathe it into your body and then back out into the environment. If you find your mind wandering to other topics, gently bring it back to this moment now, in nature, experiencing. Take in the beauty you see and feel around you. Notice how each leaf is different from the next and yet shares some common features. Appreciate the calm, quiet stability that is there in a tree, a bush, and a flower. Nature is just there, to be seen and sensed, asking nothing from you. Breathe, look, and feel grateful for the moment.

Exercise 11.2: Develop Your Compassion

You can nurture your feelings of compassion by extending kindness in the places and to the people near you. You can begin simply by taking care of the area right near where you live. Water any plants, give them nourishment if needed, and keep the area clean from trash. In caring for this little area close by, allow yourself to feel your caring for helping. Extend your compassion to pets and people in your life. As you deliberately extend small kindnesses to those around you, you may feel more compassionate feelings develop, for greater calm and comfort within.

Exercise 11.3: Pick One Thing for Gratitude

People suffering from depression sometimes have difficulty thinking of something they are grateful for. But usually most people can think of one thing, person, or situation that they can appreciate. This exercise can start a process, and is easily expanded into a weekly or daily practice.

Think about something you are grateful for in your life. Sit quietly and meditate on what you are grateful for. Let your gratitude grow as you keep your attention on being grateful.

Exercise 11.4: Gratitude List: Count Blessings, Not Burdens

A recent study (Emmons & McCullough, 2003) asked one group to make a weekly gratitude list and another group to list their hassles each week. Both groups also kept records of their moods. The researchers found that the gratitude outlook group showed higher well-being across most of the measures studied. And when the researchers had both groups make lists daily and over a longer period of time, the results were stronger.

Pick a time each day to make your own gratitude list. Write down several things you are grateful for in your life. When you are in a negative mood, you might think that you have nothing to feel thankful about in your life. But, once you start looking, you may be surprised to find that you have many things to feel grateful for. Your gratitude could come from a simple pleasure in eating a delicious cookie, from seeing a beautiful bird fly by, or even from the simple pleasure of sitting in the shade of a large tree on a warm, sunny day. You might feel grateful for certain people in your life, the education you have had, or a pet that you love. Let yourself be open to searching for these things, and you will be surprised how many you can find.

Review your gratitude list regularly and perform a meditation for each item on your list. You can do the meditation for several minutes when you first awaken and several minutes just before sleep. Return to this meditation often, especially if you find your thoughts becoming negative.

Exercise 11.5: Gratitude and Compassion in the Present Moment

It is important to keep a positive mind-set toward others, which mindfulness elicits. The following exercise is foundational for this practice.

Sit down for meditation and take a mindful inward glance. Now allow yourself to think of one thing you feel grateful for in this present moment. It might be a simple thanks for a free moment or a deep-felt feeling of gratitude toward someone in your life. Let the feeling spread through you as you keep your attention focused on gratitude here and now. Reflect on the person, contemplating that you wish them well, and inwardly hold in your thoughts that you feel thankful for the goodness that has been done. As you feel your gratitude, allow yourself to extend your compassion to that person, as he or she may have done for you. Let your feelings of caring and kindness extend to the person, and feel these emotions build within you.

Learning to Be Grateful and Compassionate Even in the Midst of Negativity

Often we are quick to criticize ourselves and hold back from recognizing our own capacities. Use meditative moments here and there, to contemplate your own qualities and abilities as well, even the simple ones. Be sure to let yourself notice positive qualities you have.

Everything in life, both the suffering and the triumphs, can be used as an opportunity to find the optimum balance for happiness and fulfillment. We often say that the problems people face can become the seeds of their potential. Anger that a client dislikes could be the source for his/her motivation; Stubbornness can be used to stubbornly stay with therapy. People don't have to escape from their own problems to find happiness. The following story illustrates this point.

Learning to Be Enlightened in Every Situation

An accomplished monk moved out of the monastery. None of the other monks could understand why such a noble enlightened monk would leave the peaceful sanctuary of monastic life. The monastery was simple

(continued)

(*continued*)

but beautiful, and all the monks treated each other with kindness and compassion.

One day a student from the monastery saw the monk shoveling dirt at a construction site. Sweat dripped from his brow and dirt was smudged all over his clothes, hands, and face. Shocked to see such a respected master engaged in a lowly activity, the student asked, "What are you doing here?"

The monk answered, "With every pile of dirt I move I am removing illusion from my mind. The dirt is my teacher."

In that moment, the student was enlightened. He realized that each action, experience, relationship—everything in life—offers an opportunity for growth, even those we might consider dirty, sweaty, or unpleasant. All experience, moment to moment, is deeply part of the continuous search for and development of enlightenment.

Everyday life can become sacred, with every action a ritual on the path. And mental health is found through living life well, even during the difficult times. Living with gratitude and compassion can help transform a suffering life to a meaningful one. The more you experience, feel, and think, the more closely immersed you can become in a happy life, if you embrace the meditative way.

Thus, negative relationships and circumstances of life don't have to be avoided but can be embraced as the ground for growth if approached correctly. Psychotherapy, when it is done well, helps clients to accept what is, as a step on their inner path of transformation. Of course, it's easy to find grounds for gratitude and compassion in the midst of fortune, success, and good relationships, but even during misfortune, poverty, and interpersonal conflict, there is the opportunity to feel grateful and compassionate.

Therefore, each situation has something to teach, if comprehended with the correct mind-set. As the Dalai Lama has explained often in his lectures and many books, anger, for example, can be overcome by realizing that even enemies bring opportunities to become wiser and more compassionate. Through the interaction, we evolve. Important insight is gained from difficult situations. We can appreciate these negative experiences and people because no positive experience could ever give us the same opportunity to transcend and grow. When we face hostility with patience, for example, we gain perseverance, while the people who lose their tempers become diminished. Any apparent outer gains they might seem to receive are unreal and deceptive, for in terms of their inner world, they have taken a step backward.

Our clients can utilize all the qualities given to them as resources on their path. Their capacity to think and feel should not be blunted but rather sharpened as a useful tool. Even interpersonal relationships can be helpful. And in the shared interpersonal experience, growth may be found for both people together.

Tibet's Buddhist monks taught that people can develop an adamantine steadfastness to maintain meditative awareness and do the right thing even in the midst of negativity. In this ability to stay on the enlightened course in every situation, people discover complete happiness and blissful joy.

Life becomes the expression of a higher, more compassionate consciousness, in which people are grateful for the multiple dimensions of life. As we have pointed out, every action, every thought, every feeling can be a teacher.

Exercise 11.6: Finding Compassion in Difficult Situations or People

Think about a situation or person who annoys you. You have probably thought a great deal about all the things that bother you about this situation or person. But have you considered what it might be doing for you? Consider the possibility that there is something you can appreciate. Perhaps you can find something to learn from this situation or person. Or maybe you have overlooked a positive aspect amid all the negativity. Let your outlook stretch to include the positive qualities you can be grateful for.

Exercise 11.7: Working through Resentment with Appreciation

Fritz Perls, the founder of Gestalt therapy, recognized the value of expressing and truly listening to both sides of conflicts. He believed that the counterpart of resentment is appreciation. This exercise can help clients work through resentment by exploring the gratitude side and, through a dialogue between resentment and gratitude, come to terms with what they resent.

Place two chairs facing each other. Sit down in one of the chairs and think about the situation or person from the last exercise, one where you feel resentment and annoyance. Express the resentments you feel about this situation/person. Now switch to the other chair and think about what you appreciate about this situation/person. You may have to dig deeper to find something you feel grateful for, but look for it. Then express that feeling and allow yourself to experience it fully. Next, switch back to the resentment chair and speak to the appreciation feelings. Switch chairs, and respond. Move back and forth between the two positions. Can you listen, from each chair, to the other position? Through a sincere, open dialogue, something new is found that incorporates both gratitude and resentment. A new perspective emerges with understanding that goes beyond each side.

GRATITUDE IN ACTION: ENGAGING BEHAVIORAL CHANGES

Just developing the feelings of gratitude starts a process. But often action speaks louder than words. Behavioral expression of gratitude and appreciation is also important for a deeper transformation. Thus, to improve generosity, "cut the knot of miserliness constricting the heart" (Mullin, 1982, p. 151) by making small changes. Begin with little easy to do things, such as sharing bits of food with a wild bird. Think of your own things you can do.

Lifestyle change begins by altering your way of living. By giving up the negative and turning toward the positive, subtle transformation takes place. Meditation brings about new perspectives—a change in consciousness. Your client will no longer feel the same way about life.

Exercise 11.8: Attuning for Benevolent Action

We busily go about our everyday lives and often do not notice the details of our immediate environment. This meditation can help your clients to be in deeper and more sensitive contact with the things around them. When they do this exercise, they will understand how meditation and action are not separate: They are one.

Begin this meditation sitting in your house (or the therapist's office). Close your eyes and visualize the environment directly outside. Do you see other houses, apartments, streets, trees, sidewalks, flowers, trashcans, signs, or people? Try to picture everything vividly. Then notice the sounds. Do you hear voices, cars, music, wind, or birds? Focus on smells. Is there the smell of automobile exhaust, grass, trees, or the aroma from a nearby restaurant? Do not just categorize or put it in words; instead just experience what is there. Meditate mindfully for several minutes on all of these sensations. Stay focused without using a label or conceptualization to describe the sensations. When you are finished, go outside and survey the area you visualized. Did you remember accurately? What did you leave out? Take a few moments to perceive carefully.

Often when people become more sensitive, they notice things they had not noticed before. You may find that you now perceive some things in your environment that you like and some that you may not like, things that you may have ignored before, or perhaps, that can be made even better. Ask yourself: Is this something that I can change? Would I like to change it myself, since I would like it even better? Perhaps you will find some small action to take to help your environment. You might decide to clean up a small area with a trash bag and rubber gloves. If your fence needs painting, perhaps it is time to devote some free time to this project. Many situations can be improved by making one small change. Often the change does not cost very much, compared to the benefit. Experiment, and then notice your response, and the effect on your personal experience. Take care of your environment, as yourself. Other people may benefit, as well—an added blessing.

Exercise 11.9: Taking Compassionate Action

Express your compassion to someone. Do something for someone else, extend a helping hand, or express kindness. It can be a simple thing, like being kind to a clerk at a store who helps or expressing sincere appreciation to a relative or friend, or it might involve doing some volunteer work to help others, which may show that you appreciate their situation. Make acts of kindness part of your daily routines when you feel moved to do them, until they become a habit. You may be pleasantly surprised to see the benefits come back to you, when you realize that you are having positive feelings of well-being and happiness for no apparent reason.

Exercise 11.10: Making Gratitude and Compassion a
Part of You with the Ideomotor Effect

You can utilize the ideomotor effect to elicit a response and thereby deepen compassion and gratitude's healing effects. (See Chapter 7 for the background on this method.)

Vividly imagine a time when you felt grateful. Or perhaps think of a situation where you felt compassion for someone who was in need and offered your help. Notice all the sensory experiences you had: what you saw, heard, felt, thought, and sensed. Hold this image in your mind as you sit comfortably. Just imagine it fully and allow your nervous system to respond. You may find that you feel more comfortable and happy. Use this exercise regularly with any of your gratitude feelings to enhance these emotions and encourage them to flourish.

CONCLUSION

We have mounting evidence that developing gratitude and compassion in clients will help in better regulation of affect and enhance attentional flexibility, both of which are vital for psychotherapeutic success. Therapists are always looking for the best ways to foster change, and there is strong evidence that introducing gratitude and compassion into therapeutic interventions can have a powerful nonspecific effect. Incorporate these simple practices into your therapy, and encourage your clients to do them between sessions.

12

Integrating Meditation into Therapy

Core Principle 12: Integrate Meditation into Most Forms of Therapy as an Adjunct or Stand-alone Method.

The object of Zen discipline [meditation] consists in acquiring a new viewpoint for looking into the essence of things.

—D. T. Suzuki

INTRODUCTION

- Introduce meditation gradually.
- Begin with short, manageable exercises such as the inward or outward glance.
- Be aware of individual client differences.
- Offer short meditations at key times during the session and between sessions.
- Use meditation with individuals, couples, families, and groups.
- Create a meditative atmosphere right in your office.
- Therapists: Take care of your own well-being with meditation.

ENHANCING THERAPEUTIC LEARNING

Meditation is a valuable tool for enhancing therapeutic learning by offering clients—and all of us—a new way to perceive directly and clearly into their deeper nature. This old Zen parable epitomizes how:

> Before I began meditation, mountains were mountains and rivers were rivers. In the midst of my meditative journey, mountains were no longer mountains and rivers were no longer rivers. Now that my meditation is complete, mountains are once again mountains and rivers are once again rivers.

Clients undergo a similar process as they proceed through therapy. At first, clients know the world through the lens of taken for granted problems that feel familiar even though they are disturbing. As the therapeutic process progresses, clients sometimes may feel defensive or uncertain as they move away from those familiar negative adjustments but haven't yet got them used to something better. Finally, when therapy is complete, things come into focus as the client has discovered new resources and a positive, fulfilling adjustment.

The Man Who Had to Go Down to Come Up

One client began therapy by telling us that he felt okay, he just had a motivation problem. Sure, he smoked a little pot, drank a six-pack of beer each day, and took some cocaine when he felt like partying (which seemed to be most evenings). But, as therapy progressed, he became aware of how intoxicated he was in his daily life. He began to question his familiar patterns and see through his defenses. He realized that his low motivation stemmed from heavy drug use, which kept him from feeling his troubling emotions. This middle period was disorienting and even threatening at times. But he endured the discomforts associated with facing his deeper issues and learning to accept himself and go from there. By the end of treatment, he could embrace the full range of his emotional experiencing and find joy without drugs. His awareness sharpened as he perceived things more realistically. Once again, mountains were mountains and rivers were rivers, and he had the clarity of vision to truly see them as they were.

Meditation can be easily integrated into traditional forms of psychotherapy. This chapter instructs on preliminaries for bringing meditation into therapy. The techniques you will use can draw on the focus, open-focus, and no-focus meditations taught throughout this multimedia package. All of these skills are cornerstones for helping people overcome psychological problems by becoming more balanced, aware, and attuned to the flow of life.

INTRODUCING MEDITATION

Introduce meditation to clients gently and gradually. Keeping in mind the importance of nonspecific factors for therapeutic healing, offer a meditation that is manageable for your client. In some of our talks, participants have told us that they feel frustrated when clients could not sustain meditation for 15 to 30 minutes as they did and so gave up using it as part of therapy. We have found that it is especially difficult for people who are having emotional disturbance to sustain meditation for long periods. But they can do it for a short time. So, begin briefly, starting with a minute or less. Even a single minute can have a profound effect. We had an adult client with ADHD (attention-deficit hyperactivity disorder) who found it a great triumph when he could focus for 10 seconds. The feeling of mastery he gained gave him confidence to redouble his efforts. He built on that mastery experience to sustain focus for longer periods. Invite success and skills will build.

How long you spend doing meditation with clients during the session depends on how fully you want to integrate it into your approach. At the very least, have clients perform some of the exercises for several minutes per session. You can begin with the one-minute inward glance to help people come to the session fully. We have also done this meditation following deep work to help clients gather themselves and take note of what has occurred. And we sometimes use this meditation at the end of the session to allow clients to consolidate and gather themselves before they leave. Ending sessions with a sense of well-being can be a strong reinforcement to motivate clients to return.

Exercise 12.1: The One-Minute Inward Glance

While sitting here now, close your eyes and turn your attention to your body. Notice how your body feels sitting in the chair. Sense the air as it touches your skin and the light on your eyelids. Let your attention scan through your body to notice anything else that occurs to you. Next, notice what you are feeling as you sit here with me in the office. Notice the kinds of feelings you are having now. They might change as you pay attention. Finally, what are you thinking? What kinds of thoughts are running through your mind? Don't get caught up in any one thought, but instead notice the kinds of thoughts that flow past. Now take a moment to simply pay attention to whatever you notice, grounded in this moment.

Exercise 12.2: The One-Minute Outward Glance

If you have clients who are working on painful inner conflicts, such that turning attention inward might be disturbing, you can have them turn attention outwards, for a one-minute outward glance. We often do so with depressed clients or people suffering from obsessive thoughts. And you can use only one modality for centering, such as awareness of the body, without using other modalities for focus. Always individualize practice to the needs of clients.

Turn your mindful attention outward. Look around the room and allow your attention to notice what draws your interest, but stay aware of the process. Stay in the present moment, perhaps even saying to yourself, now I notice the chair; now I am looking at the painting; now I see a pattern in the painting; now I am drawn to the blue colors; now I notice the calm atmosphere … Stay with your experience of what is around you as each new moment unfolds, to get a sense of how you experience your surroundings right now.

After helping with the direction of attention, it is good to gently encourage clients to freely explore what emerges and follow the therapeutic path to wherever it leads, but with patience. Therapeutic understanding takes time. Often it is like a jigsaw puzzle, where various further insights are necessary to form a meaningful, coherent whole picture. Be willing to permit patterns to form and re-form in meaningful ways as experiences evolve.

RECOGNIZE INDIVIDUAL DIFFERENCES

Everyone has tendencies. Your clients' reactions to the exercises might be different from your own. The meditations you experienced as easy may instead be experienced as the most difficult ones for your client. But the meditations you might find difficult to do might be the ones your client likes best. Some people find that paying attention to the body is easier to do than visualizing. For others, it is the reverse. You may find some clients can clear their minds easily but have difficulty focusing. Others may have an easy time being mindful, but can't keep attention steadily focused on one thing no matter how they try. There is no standardized correct set of potentials that clients bring to the session, but as you use these techniques, your experience will teach you what is typical and what is not.

Sample each type of meditation in order to familiarize yourself with a broad range of methods. Doing so will allow you to guide your clients toward the best ways to address their individuality.

TIMING MEDITATION PRACTICE BETWEEN SESSIONS

Encourage clients to practice between sessions. This extends the therapeutic influence into their week. You can give clients different exercises each week, drawn from the many in this multimedia package. Pick what will facilitate the processes you are working on in the sessions.

Help clients find a time of day for meditation and a simple posture routine that fits their personality and schedule and helps in reducing resistance. First thing in the morning is good for early risers; evening practice usually suits night owls. But sometimes, contrast with the usual routine helps get around resistance.

Start with the amount of time, perhaps a few minutes, that is possible for clients to master. When working on a problem, ask clients to meditate for one or two minutes, but do it several times each day. They will extend the time as they are able. Encourage them to take brief mindful glances throughout the day. These are one-minute mindfulness breaks to observe meditating in different contexts. Suggest that clients keep a journal to note down the experience and its meaning.

USE MEDITATION WITH INDIVIDUALS, COUPLES, FAMILIES, AND GROUPS

You can use meditation with individual clients in sessions and between sessions. But you can also introduce meditation with couples, adding a nonverbal dimension that brings partners together for a profound experience of sharing. If you perform group therapy, you can easily add meditation as part of regular group therapy, couples, and family sessions.

Traditionally, meditation was performed in groups, and you can use meditation methods for group therapy as well. Meditation has been researched with large groups (Rausch, Gramling, & Auerbach, 2006). Data collected from a group of experiments that have come to be known as *the Maharishi Effect* (Abou-Nader, Alexander, & Davies, 1990) found that after many days of group meditation, violent crime in the community actually decreased. And so we have good evidence that meditation can be effective with groups for enhancing peace and harmony. Therapists will find it a helpful adjunct for couples, group, and family therapy. It can also be used in the classroom (Langer, 1989) and with organizations.

People enjoy sharing meditation. The wordless experience can bring a couple, families, or groups closer together. You will also find that when people share in meditation, they will find it easier to be open and share their experiences more generally. You may also want to add group sessions strictly devoted to meditation for your individual clients.

CREATING A MEDITATIVE ATMOSPHERE

You can add to clients' experiences by creating a bit of atmosphere in your office. Even a subtle touch indirectly suggests calm awareness to clients. You might create a meditation corner. Place two meditation pillows on the floor, one for you and the other for your client. Add some simple decoration, such as a single flower in a vase or a picture on the wall, that suggests meditation.

Even if you don't have enough room to add anything new, you can burn incense or dim the lights slightly. Our sense of smell goes directly from the nose to the brain, so a gentle aroma can add an immediate atmosphere. Most important is your invitation, which welcomes your clients to join in a meditative moment.

MEDITATION FOR THERAPISTS

The power of meditation comes through experience. Therefore, if you would like to use meditation with clients, we recommend experiencing it personally. Develop a personal practice of your own. Then you will be better able to help your clients to use these methods. Add some meditation into your daily routines.

The therapeutic relationship is one of the most important nonspecific factors that make psychotherapy effective. Jerome Frank and his team at

Johns Hopkins did a 25-year follow up study on what makes therapy effective (Frank & Frank, 1991). They found that certain factors that were not specific to any one form of therapy but were present in all effective therapy had a strong influence on therapeutic efficacy. The key factors were faith, hope, positive expectancy, experiences of mastery, having a therapeutic rationale, and the therapeutic relationship. Therefore, your therapeutic presence is important. Taking time for your own self-care can make a significant difference in your outcomes. A short meditation session can help you find your center and feel in touch and at ease. This will affect your clients deeply. So, please practice these methods yourself, between clients and at various times during your week.

Therapists and educators who meditate are less likely to experience burnout and tend to stay inspired about their work, keeping what is known in meditation as "beginner mind"— the enthusiasm of a beginner with heightened awareness and deep empathy—enhancing their expertise. Sometimes, during sessions, we listen to heart-wrenching stories of abuse, disasters, deaths, wars, and violence. We share in the suffering in order to help our clients navigate their dark, stormy journeys. As sensitive and empathic listeners, we resonate with them at times, feeling painful emotions of our own within. The word *burnout* implies being used up and spent. But burning also implies a certain passion, and often those people who suffer from burnout are the very ones who were most excited and enthusiastic when they first started practicing psychotherapy (Korunka, Tement, Zdrehus, & Borza, 2010). If you are suffering from burnout, meditation can help you. We encourage you to take note of your difficulty, meditate regularly, and learn from the effects. You might be pleasantly surprised how a short daily meditation session can turn the tide and bring you back to your original beginner's mind, to once again be passionate and enthusiastic about your profession.

CONCLUSION

Whether you use meditation as a primary intervention or a supplementary tool, you will find these methods to be helpful with a broad range of clients. By teaching your clients to meditate, you give them a skill they can take home to use between sessions and a path to follow that will help them find direction for their life, so they can become attuned, calm, alert, and aware.

13

Meditations for Stress

Core Principle 13: Meditation Alters the Physical, Emotional, and Cognitive Components of Stress. Practice It to Calm, Manage, and Relieve Stress.

Nothing is missing. You have everything you need.
—Paraphrased from Zen master Lin Chi (died 866)

INTRODUCTION

- Focus on softening the breath.
- Focus on a calm experience.
- Turn around negative judgments mindfully.
- Open focus on compassion.
- Mindful walking to let go of stress.
- No-focus mind clearing for a stress-free moment.

BEGIN WITH CALMING TO LOWER THE NERVOUS SYSTEM STRESS RESPONSE

Zen master Lin Chi was correct when he said that we have everything we need. The nervous system is built to handle threat. We have a finely tuned capacity to respond to danger by means of our natural stress pathway, a specific group of areas, known as the Hypothalamic-Pituitary-Adrenal Axis. When this is activated, a cascade of protective responses is triggered that helps us to cope with danger and then return to rest. During threat, the autonomic nervous system shifts. Sympathetic arousal helps awaken our resources to deal with the threat. After the threat has passed, the hypothalamus signals the parasympathetic nervous system, lowering arousal, which returns the organism to normal, to balance. When functioning well, this pathway is fluid and responsive, moving seamlessly from alert to relaxed.

But often we get out of tune with our natural capacities, especially in the midst of challenging, ongoing circumstances. Sometimes the threat persists or we experience it as if it is continuing. Or our resources are severely taxed, trying to cope. The activation of the HPA pathway may persist and the stress becomes problematic. According to a report by the American Psychological Association (2008), most mental disorders place extra demands on the nervous system, thereby keeping the body in an overly activated stress condition that adds to the negative effect. Therefore, treating stress will not only help return the nervous system to balance but will also help in easing most psychological disorders. People can learn how to manage this natural nervous system pathway and balance their responses so that the reaction can work to their benefit.

Meditation offers tangible tools known to influence the brain's fear/stress pathway. Researchers propose that the special focus of attention is helpful for better toleration of stress (Vaitl & Ott, 2005). When meditation methods drawn from Kundalini yoga were used to try to lower stress, subjects showed improvement on physiological measures, indicating that they had successfully lowered the stress response of their nervous system (Granath, Ingvarsson, von Thiele, & Lundberg, 2006). Meditation enhances the ability to listen accurately to nervous system signals and reduce the stress response to manageable levels when it is overly extreme. Then it becomes possible to cope with life situations better with improved attitudes and more positive adaptive appraisals of themselves, in their circumstances. In addition, by addressing stressful situations well, clients will initiate a healing process to help other problems they might be working on.

Exercise 13.1: Breath Meditation: Focus on Softening the Breath

Breathing meditations can have a profound calming effect on mind and brain. As discussed in Chapter 8, research shows that breathing meditations activate the vagus nerve and the parasympathetic nervous system for calming. Thus, meditative breath is a direct way to calm emotions and relax the body. You can use any of the breathing meditations presented in this book. This next classic breathing exercise works directly to bring about calming, by gently softening each breath while staying focused and aware. Encourage the client to perform this exercise at different times throughout the day and evening, even if for just a few minutes each time, to elicit the natural ability we all have to feel relaxed and calm. And this is important: Elicit calmness, but do not try to make your client feel calm. Forced calmness is superficial. Seek the deeper tranquility within.

Sit on a pillow on the floor in a balanced sitting position with your legs crossed. Or, if sitting on the floor is not comfortable for you, sit in an upright chair, letting your feet rest flat on the floor. In either position, find a relaxed, upright position with your back relatively straight so that your breathing passages can be unobstructed. Place your hands on your rib cage and feel them move in and out with each breath. When your attention is fairly well focused on breathing, remove your hands and allow your breathing to soften. Draw air in gently and smoothly, not too fast or too slow, and then let it softly and smoothly out. Stay aware of the whole process, noticing the movement of your rib cage and the feeling of the air moving in and out. There is no need to force or hold your breath. Instead, just breathe gently and comfortably as you keep your focus directed to each breath. Your breathing will be natural and light, but slightly slower than normal. Keep your attention focused on your breathing and sustain this for several minutes, working up to 10 or more minutes.

Exercise 13.2: Drawing on Your Ability to Be Calm:
Focus on a Calm Experience

Everyone has had times in their lives when they have felt at ease and calm. Even those who are chronically depressed or anxious can recall isolated moments when they felt relaxed for a brief time. These experiences are inner resources. It is possible to draw on these past experiences to help develop calmness now in meditation. The next exercise will help to find calmness through memory. By vividly imagining, you activate the mind-body ideomotor link described in Chapter 7.

Close your eyes. Let your mind think back to some time or place when you felt very relaxed and at ease. Choose one particular experience. Recall the details. Did it have a distinctive smell, such as the aroma of pine trees in a forest, salt air at the ocean, leather and books in a beloved library? Notice other details. Was there a gentle breeze, warm sun, or even brisk cold? Look around and imagine that you are right there. As you move around or sit in this place and time, observe what you feel. Your muscles will tend to relax. Allow this to occur naturally. When you are finished, return to the present time and place, relaxed and refreshed. Allow the experience to linger, contemplating deeply.

STRESS MANAGEMENT

How people manage or cope with stress has a large effect on how uncomfortable they feel. Management of stress begins at the level of attitudes. Often people complain about feeling stressed and make it worse by their negative assessments of its meaning to them. Mindfulness, with its practice of setting aside judgments, can help people let go of these harmful patterns while adopting a more neutral, accepting attitude. Use the mindfulness meditations in this book to foster the process of accepting through open-minded awareness.

Exercise 13.3: Turn around Negative Judgments Mindfully

Begin by sitting comfortably and relaxing for a minute. Now take a step back from your usual thoughts about your stress and mindfully notice what you are experiencing right now. Do you hear an undercurrent of negative thoughts, such as "I'm really stressed!" or "How awful this situation is!" or "Other people are bothering me." Notice mindfully whatever you are thinking as your thoughts flow by, remaining neutrally aware moment by moment. Can you remain poised in the center, setting aside your judgment of your experience as good or bad? Simply let your focus of attention survey all your experiencing. Perhaps you also notice other thoughts, feelings, or sensations, such as experiencing excitement, alertness, or challenge. Stay neutrally aware as you breathe comfortably in and out. You may find that your experience shifts as you feel in balance and attuned to whatever occurs.

Exercise 13.4: Open Focus on Compassion

Deliberately fostering a more positive stance toward stress will help in its management. This exercise develops compassion. You can also use the gratitude exercises in Chapter 11.

Take a moment to allow yourself to focus on compassion. Is there a more compassionate way to view your situation or the other people who are involved? Begin by reflecting on your usual response to stress, then ask inwardly, "Does this reaction bring about harmony, peaceful resolution, and better coping in myself or in the others? Or am I eliciting disharmony, discomfort, and poorer coping?" Expand your point of view to include others' feelings, and their situation. Put yourself in the other person's shoes and ask yourself, "How would I feel in their situation? Could I be more compassionate and understanding towards them?" Notice your experiencing now, as you consider a more sympathetic and caring perspective. You may find that your discomfort eases.

LETTING STRESS GO

People can practice meditations that will lead to a lowering of stress. These techniques relax the nervous system for a calmer adjustment. Begin with short meditation sessions because stressed individuals often find it difficult to stop and meditate. Even a brief meditation can start a process of letting stress go.

Exercise 13.5: Mindful Walking to Let Go of Stress

When feeling stressed some clients, especially those who feel anxious as well, may find that sitting still is difficult. Traditionally Zen monks would intersperse their long day of sitting meditation with walking meditation.

Using mindfulness methods you practiced in Chapter 10, stand up and begin walking slowly. Hold your hands together, palms touching, or else let your arms swing naturally at your sides. Walk slowly, with awareness on every step. Pay attention to how your foot meets the ground. Notice how your weight shifts from foot to foot. Keep your breathing and your body relaxed as you walk slowly. Focus your attention on walking. If your mind starts to fill with thoughts about things other than walking, stop and wait as you bring your mind back to awareness of standing. Then, when you feel that your thoughts are clear, begin walking again. Maintain awareness of every step with a quiet mind. When you feel ready to stop, just stand for a minute or two, quietly aware in the moment.

Exercise 13.6: No-Focus Mind Clearing for a Stress-Free Moment

Now that your client has reduced stress and cleared the mind while moving, you can guide him/her to expand into another way, without the necessity for movement.

Begin by simply sitting comfortably and not thinking about anything in particular. If a thought or wish arises, bring it to awareness, and consider the thought or wish as it is. Don't evaluate it. Simply observe that it is, just as you did when performing mindfulness meditations. Then, when you feel that you have given the thought or wish enough consideration, you will feel ready to allow it to leave and return to not thinking about anything. When doing this, you will begin to become aware of your natural rhythm of shifting from thinking to not thinking. Gradually, your thoughts slow down a bit. Eventually your mind will clear, leaving calm consciousness free of stress, simply open in this present moment.

CONCLUSION

Stress is an experience that can be affected in many ways. The exercises you have participated in have opened up a very direct means of bringing about a transformation in mind and body. And, this meditative change is not just restricted to what is taking place in the moment of meditating. The change from meditation begins a process that will lower stress and promote well-being.

14

Meditative Regulation of Emotions

Core Principle 14: The Paradox of Meditative Regulation Is That You Gain Control by Letting Go.

The purpose is to see things as they are, to observe things as they are, and to let everything go as it goes. This is to put everything under control in its widest sense.
—Shunryu Suzuki, Zen Mind, Beginner Mind

INTRODUCTION

- Whole body breathing to stabilize the nervous system.
- Focus on breathing to initiate awareness of emotions.
- Observe emotions mindfully.
- Embrace feelings.
- Practice healing compassion and forgiveness.

People regulate their emotions differently. For example, some people dissociate from their emotions by narrowing their perceptual field. Others have trouble noticing or even knowing what they feel. Some explode with feelings while others avoid, especially when feelings are uncomfortable (Braboszcz, Habnusseau, & Delorme, 2010). The intensity varies as well: Some people experience emotions strongly and others, only weakly. People take on certain attitudes and fears about their emotions, such as being afraid the emotion will never end, fearing that they will lose control, dreading the judgment of others, and worrying that the body sensations they feel could be a disease. These emotional styles often become expressed in the different psychological disorders we treat in therapy. In fact, most mental disorders have a component of these styles and attitudes toward emotions.

Research shows that meditation helps people to regulate affect better (Lutz, Brefczynski-Lewis, Johnstone, & Davidson, 2008a). What people find is that by meditating on their emotions, they discover a natural way to regulate that fits their natural tendencies. They experience certain rewards from meditative regulation: Emotions are quieted, troubling feelings are better understood, and a different, more regulated balance is found.

But the way that meditation brings about better emotional regulation may seem paradoxical at first, because letting go while in the meditative state is the way to gain control. People often think that the best way to control their emotions is to become a personal drill sergeant, suppressing negative feelings. Clients are often fighting against themselves, rejecting some qualities while wishing for others. Their energy becomes erratic and their lives out of balance. But this seems to them to be the only alternative to losing control and blurting out their emotions.

The ancient wisdom of meditation offers a far more effective way to self-regulate, through the fine art of letting be. Meditative awareness of emotions as they occur leads back to a natural center of balance. In a sense, by accepting feelings as they are and letting them be, without being swept into a wave of emotion, clients find a new source of regulation: their natural attunement to their deeper nature. This chapter offers a meditative approach to affect regulation that you can use with clients who are struggling with aggression, anger, sadness, and other troubling emotions.

With your guidance, clients can safely explore the dark waters of their deepest fears in ways that might not be as available to them without the objectivity and balanced calm that they can develop in meditation. Through the meditative process, they undergo a transformation that puts them in touch with resources of their personality that can help them do this.

Emotions become easier to accept and handle, and paradoxically, their intensity often diminishes. These meditations will help people develop their ability to stabilize emotions, even when strongly aroused, and gain the control they need to feel and do better in their lives.

BEGIN BY RELAXING THROUGH BREATHING

Exercise 14.1: Soften the Breath to Stabilize the Nervous System

Learning to free your breathing and allow it to flow through the whole body calms the nervous system to moderate emotional reactions to some extent. Thus, through meditative breathing, clients can experience temporary moments of calm even when they are dealing with uncomfortable emotions. This practice sets in motion a calmer adjustment and offers hope to clients that they can begin to feel better. Breathing meditations can be a helpful step on the path to regulating emotions. You can draw upon the many breathing meditations found throughout this book as well as guide your client to relax by breathing with the whole body.

Stand comfortably in your bare feet, socks, or slippers, with your feet approximately shoulder width apart. Close your eyes and breathe comfortably. Follow the air as it goes in through your nose and down into your lungs. Imagine that with each breath in, the air penetrates through your entire body, softening and relaxing throughout. With each exhalation, tensions are released from head to toe.

Next, raise your hands lightly over your head while you breathe in, expanding your rib cage slightly as it fills with air. Let your arms drop back gently to your sides as you breathe out. Breaths and movements should be soft. Repeat several times.

LEARN ABOUT FEELINGS THROUGH
MEDITATIVE AWARENESS

People often try to escape their moods, change them, or avoid them. Paradoxically, one of the most effective ways to be calmer and less volatile is to embrace the mood or emotion, to feel it fully and become one with it. In this way, people come to know more about themselves. This awareness opens the opportunity to learn from the feeling.

Exercise 14.2: Focus on Breathing When Feeling an Emotion

Breathing is intimately linked to emotions. When people are emotionally aroused, breathing rate alters. People who are out of touch with their emotions or those who find emotions difficult to handle may begin the attuning process by turning attention to breathing.

Sit quietly at a time when you are having an emotion and turn your attention to breathing. Notice how your rib cage moves in and out as you breathe. Scan for any tightness that you might be having as you follow each breath, in and out. Do you notice any patterns, such as quick, short breaths or tight rib cage? Observe mindfully, without judging these patterns as good or bad. Instead, simply notice. As each moment passes, you may observe that the pattern changes, perhaps relaxing or slowing. Breathe and observe, accepting your experience just as it is. You might find that your emotion becomes easier to handle as you get to know and accept non-judgmentally the breathing patterns associated with it.

Exercise 14.3: Open-Focus Mindful Observation of Emotions

In mindfulness meditation, learn to watch your thoughts from the objective, unbiased vantage point of your inner mind. Then you can transfer this meditative ability of observation to observing your emotions. Perform this exercise at different times of the day, when you are feeling different emotions.

Sit comfortably. Turn your attention inward, away from the outer world. Notice details of your physical experience, your sensations. Is your heartbeat gentle and comfortable, or is it quick and pressured? Does your skin feel warm, cool, or clammy? Where? Are your muscles tight, sore, relaxed, or loose? Notice whether you feel any anxiety or tightness in your chest and stomach. What is it like? And finally, do you notice a feeling, such as happy, content, sad, tired, annoyed? Observe the physical sensations associated with the emotions you feel. Do not attempt to alter or evaluate your emotional state; simply observe it in every aspect possible, just as it is. Notice the experience but try not to become lost in it; retain your vantage point of detached observer, as in previous exercises, sitting on the banks of the stream rather than being swept along with the current.

Continue in this way. If an emotion arises, bring it to consciousness; notice it just as it is with its corresponding sensations or thoughts. But don't evaluate it or tell yourself how bad it feels. Simply observe what you feel objectively in this moment. Then observe what you feel in the next moment. In doing this, you will begin to become aware of a change in your feeling tone. Gradually, your thoughts will clear and feelings will settle, as you handle your emotions more comfortably.

Exercise 14.4: No-Focus Embrace Your Feeling Exercise

Now that you have observed your emotions, close your eyes again for a further meditation. Sit comfortably. Allow yourself to accept the emotion fully. If you are feeling sad, let the emotion spread through you. Let it be, do not try to alter it, but if the emotional tone spontaneously changes, allow it to happen. Embrace it, accept it, be one with it. Thus, be sadness if you are sad, with no separation between you and your sadness. Do not add to it or draw conclusions. Simply allow the feeling to be, and wait. It may seem paradoxical to accept an emotion you might wish would go away, but through this very process, you will find that the emotion shifts, perhaps softens, or transforms in healing ways. Trust yourself and allow the process to unfold.

DEVELOP HEALING COMPASSION AND FORGIVENESS

Often when people suffer emotionally, they feel angry at themselves or others. Developing compassion and forgiveness can pave the way for healing.

Psychologists have long recognized how a social feeling for others is an inherent trait in the healthy personality. Alfred Adler, one of Sigmund Freud's great disciples, once said, "Empathy and understanding are facts of social feeling, of harmony with the universe" (Adler & Deutsch, 1959, p. 43). A healthy and happy adjustment often generalizes into a positive feeling for others. Compassion will grow when planted in the fertile soil of health. Meditations can enhance feelings of compassion so that it becomes a natural expression of living.

After your client is engaged in the process of self-acceptance, you can begin to help him or her extend this sense of acceptance toward others. The next meditation can teach how to develop a compassionate attitude, based on acceptance, motivated from within.

Exercise 14.5: Open Focus on Compassion for Others

Often people who are bothered by emotions such as anger are holding on to resentments. But perpetuating resentments tends to fuel their uncomfortable feelings. The Dalai Lama tradition teaches that holding on to anger hurts the person who holds the resentment far more than the person to whom the anger is directed. Meditations were developed to help people free themselves of long-standing anger and resentment, opening the potential for an experience of inner peace.

This type of meditation comes from a long tradition, first practiced by the first and third Dalai Lamas. They called them the lojang teachings, a way to develop compassion. The current Dalai Lama believes these teachings have been essential in his personal development:

> I myself received the lojang teachings when still a child, and have used them as the basis for my practice since that time. I include lojang methods of meditation for cultivating the spirit of love and compassion in my own daily devotions and have greatly benefited from them.
> **—The Dalai Lama (in Druppa 1993, p. 13)**

The lojang method can teach how to develop compassion for the people in your clients' lives, even people with whom they feel angry.

First think of neutral people in your life: those who you do not know personally and who have neither helped nor hurt you in any way. Try to generate a feeling of calm and composure about them. Can you allow yourself to feel kindness and compassion for them? This probably will not be too difficult. Next, try imagining someone you are very close to. Allow yourself to develop a calm, composed attitude toward this person. Then, let yourself extend feelings of kindness and compassion toward them. Finally, think about someone who has angered you. Can you allow yourself to feel calm composure about him or her? This may be more difficult, but keep in mind that harboring anger, even toward those who have angered you, hurts you. Gently allow yourself to let go of this anger and develop your own calm within. If possible, can you extend this calm feeling toward them? This might involve forgiving them for what they have done to you. Often when someone has done wrong, they are suffering themselves. As you consider this possibility, you may be able to feel compassion for their suffering. Eventually you may even be able to extend feelings of kindness toward them. This emotional skill develops with practice, but as you stop holding resentments toward others, you will find yourself feeling greater well-being and comfort in your life.

CONCLUSION

Cognitive methods engage the deliberate use of the thinking centers of the brain to help calm emotions for improved emotional regulation. Meditation can enhance these efforts by offering an additional approach that attunes to what is and allows it to be, using objective awareness. The understandings gained by becoming accurately in touch with emotional responses will add a helpful dimension to cognitive regulation. In addition, clients gain a deeper sense of their own emotional needs and feelings so that they can heal old wounds and move forward by embracing the broader perspective of compassion.

15

Meditations for Depression

Core Principle 15: Meditation Can Help to Activate
a Depressed Nervous System, Transforming
Negative Rumination into Broader Awareness
and Deeper Compassion.

---

*I believe that every one of us has the basis to be happy, to access the warm
and compassionate states of mind that bring happiness.*

—The Dalai Lama

INTRODUCTION

- Focus on the complete breath to activate energy.
- Activate energy by meditation on the lower abdomen.
- Visualize movement to enhance energy.
- Turn attention meditatively outward.
- Four steps to change negative judgments of self and others.
- Forgive through recognition of suffering.
- Develop gratitude.
- Allow well-being.

As the Dalai Lama stated, happiness has the capacity to be happy. In fact, we are wired to be happy, with neurotransmitters that are released when we experience enjoyment. When clients are unhappy, something is out of balance. Part of the process of alleviating the reaction of depression involves deconstructing, thereby taking away whatever interferes with the natural balance of mind and brain.

Untying the Knots of Depression

Buddha explained this principle to his disciple Ananda. He tied a knot in a silk handkerchief and asked Ananda, "What is this?"

Ananda answered, "A knot."

Then Buddha tied another knot and asked, "What is this?" Ananda answered, "Another knot."

He continued to do this until he had six knots, and each time Ananda answered the same way. Buddha said, "When I showed you the first knot you called it a knot, and when I showed you the second, and third, and so on you still insisted they were all knots."

Ananda was confused and asked, "Why do you imply I am incorrect to say that these are knots?"

Buddha answered, "The handkerchief is one whole, one piece of woven silk. By my tying knots in it, nothing has changed except its appearance. It is still a handkerchief."

Source: Paraphrased from the *Surangama Sutra* in Low (2000, p. 137).

Depression manifests in distinctive nervous system patterns that disrupt the natural capacity to feel enjoyment. Neural imaging reveals that the depressed brain is underactivated and has lower levels of the excitatory neurotransmitter glutamate as well as dysregulation in serotonin (which leads to moodiness) and in norepinephrine (which usually lowers energy). Thus, raising energy levels with breathing and movement meditations can be a helpful component in combating depression.

The neurological influence on depression is evident. And yet you might wonder, which comes first, the neurological state or the experience of feeling depressed? Cognitive theories of depression credit a negative view of the self and dysfunctional attitudes as the underlying causes that set the symptoms and neurological reactions in motion (Abela & D'Alessandro, 2002). Research shows that the ways that meditation clears away negative self-appraisals and fosters nonjudgmental awareness can be a powerful tool for altering the symptoms of depression and the cognitive components of the pattern.

This chapter provides meditations that can help in the treatment of depression. You can use them alongside conventional psychotherapy and medication or as a stand-alone treatment. You will find a two-pronged approach: First we address the nervous system imbalances through calming meditations combined with gentle activations for mind and brain. Next we give meditative ways to overcome low self-esteem, negative thinking, anger, and resentment. All of these meditations are variations of the focus, open-focus, and no-focus methods in Part III. Feel free to adapt and modify them for the unique needs of your clients.

ACTIVATE THE ENERGY AND CALM THE MIND

Meditation can help to regulate feelings of vitality and calm. Restoring the balance of the flow of energy meditatively can help clients with depression activate their nervous system. As their energy rises, clients will feel better and be more motivated and able to work on the issues behind their depression.

Exercise 15.1: Focus on the Complete Breath to Raise Energy

Drawn from yoga pranayama practice, the complete breath helps free the breathing passages, giving the maximum benefit from a minimum expenditure of energy. The breath should not be forced but rather gently allowed. Then tensions around the breathing passages ease, and breathing can be unhindered and natural.

Stand comfortably, but as straight as possible without straining. Turn your attention to your breathing. Breathe in steadily through your nose. Allow air to fill the upper section of your lungs by letting your diaphragm expand. Let the air move down into the middle part of your lungs, pushing out the lower ribs and chest. Draw the air all the way down into the lower part of your abdomen, allowing it to expand. Do so in one smooth inhalation, permitting your chest cavity to expand in all directions. Let your rib cage, diaphragm, and abdomen relax with the breath as the air fills you. Retain the breath for a few seconds. Then exhale very slowly, beginning from the abdomen. Draw your abdomen in gently, lifting it slightly, letting your diaphragm tighten as the air leaves your lungs. Let your ribs draw together as you exhale. Keep your attention focused on your body as the air flows in and out.

Exercise 15.2: Focus on Abdominal Breathing to Stimulate Energy

The Qigong meditation traditions of China viewed the abdomen as the source for energy regulation. Internal energy or chi corresponds to the Greek word *pneuma* and the Sanskrit word *prana,* meaning breath, respiration, wind, vital spirit, and soul. Being flexible and relaxed allows chi to flow smoothly. But when chi is blocked, people become ill or emotionally disturbed. The meditative interpretation of the lowered activation found in depression is that it is a result of blocked chi. Meditations that release chi will help restore balance to bring emotional healing. Breathing is one of the premier methods for unblocking chi to allow it to circulate as it should. Perform these meditations gently and regularly to bring about a lasting change.

You might find it easier to experience your breathing more fully by placing your hands lightly over your abdomen. You should feel an in-and-out movement in your abdomen as the air enters and leaves. You do not need to take deep breaths. Simply keep your breathing as natural as possible and try to stay relaxed throughout.

Keep your attention on your lower abdomen as you continue to breathe comfortably. Bring the air in through your nose, down into your lungs, and then out again. Permit your rib cage to rise and fall slightly, and your abdomen to expand and contract with each complete breath in and out. Breathe gently, as you focus all your attention on your lower abdomen. Do you begin to feel slight warmth or tingling there? Whether you do or not, imagine warmth or tingling and then let it spread. Imagine that it circles around to your back, up through your head, and then back down again to your abdomen. Keep your attention moving in this circle through your body. With practice, you will be able to feel a warm tingling, your internal energy.

Exercise 15.3: Visualize Movement to Raise Energy

There is an ancient Chinese saying that where attention goes, chi flows. One ancient meditation method for raising energy is to mindfully imagine movement without actually moving. By directing attention toward imagined movement, surprisingly, energy levels will rise almost as if one has actually moved. This exercise is particularly helpful for depression, where people may find it easier to imagine movement than actually moving, and still get benefits. This meditation can serve as a springboard to regular exercise.

Stand and place your feet shoulder width apart, arms at your sides. Relax your body. Imagine slowly bending your knees and allowing your arms to hang down as you inhale gently. Imagine your breath moving down into your legs and arms. Then vividly picture yourself slowly and evenly straightening your legs as you imagine raising your arms up over your head, fully extended and exhale, imagining the air flowing around your body and out. Now inhale as you imagine lowering yourself down, moving your arms back down to your sides as you bend your knees. Once again imagine the air flowing into your limbs. Slowly exhale as you imagine straightening your knees again and raising your arms overhead. Repeat, inhaling as you imagine moving down, exhaling as you imagine moving up. Maintain loose, slow, smooth gentle breathing, vividly picturing the air flowing through your entire body. Do you feel tingling or warmth? Let yourself feel energy flow through you.

OVERCOMING NEGATIVE MOOD

Depression often stems from low self-esteem along with feelings of resentment and anger towards the self and others. Emphasis is often on negative thoughts and feelings, activating the right amygdala, which processes negative emotions. In fact, many depressed clients have an overactivation in the right amygdala as they filter their experience through a distorted lens that only perceives the negative in their lives. Meditation can shift the balance toward well-being and happiness. Research shows that people who practiced compassion meditation deactivated their right amygdala and activated the left amygdala while also showing lowering on depression scales (Desbordes, Negi, Pace, Wallace, Raison, & Schwartz, 2012). These meditation exercises guide in this process, to help your depressed clients gently overcome their negativity and discover their positive resources within.

Exercise 15.4: Turn Attention Meditatively Outward

Sometimes, when people feel hopeless, gloomy, and despairing, the inward focus of attention tends to make things worse. A shift in attentional focus can help clients turn attention away from ruminating and out toward the greater world, hopefully. You can initiate this process of turning toward more positive expectations by guiding your clients to turn attention outward. This exercise teaches how to meditate on an outer object of focus. Find the direction of focus that is associated with the mood, to discern how to intervene through attention.

Pick something beautiful in the room or perhaps outdoors. Focus your attention fully on it. Notice all the details. If any other thoughts arise, notice them mindfully, without judgment, and then gently bring your attention back to the object of focus. Return to this meditation regularly to initiate a new habit directing attention to the outer world.

Extend this exercise between sessions by turning attention to observe your surroundings in various environments. You might begin by looking around you in a particular room of your house or observing carefully as you take a walk outside. Notice everything around you: the objects you find there and interesting qualities, such as colors, textures, shapes. Observe mindfully, without deciding whether you like what you see or not. Simply observe and let yourself perceive deeply. Look for an even broader scope, perhaps gazing out toward the horizon to take in as much of the environment as you can see. Breathe comfortably as you look, and let yourself truly see what is there.

Exercise 15.5: Four Steps to Change Negative Judgments of Self and Others

Attunement itself is the center of focus, not what you attune to, for example, whether it is opinions or concepts of others or yourself. Attend to the process of attunement in this exercise, not the content. This is one of the keys to mood change. As discussed in earlier chapters, negative judgment of self and others can interfere with clear, objective perception.

Step One: *As you turn your attention to a significant person in your life, perhaps you feel negative thoughts emerge. Begin by noting that you are thinking about this person, and then observing what you are thinking about this person. Notice the tone. Are you judging them negatively?*

Step Two: *Question your assessment. Does it include all the facts? Perhaps you are overlooking other qualities and interactions that may not have been that negative, or even had some positive or helpful qualities.*

Step Three: *Now imagine an interaction with this person that was not negative—perhaps focus on a positive quality this person has expressed in another context, such as being kind to animals, or being organized, or being strong. You may need to expand your perception to find something positive, but everyone has some strengths or virtues if you look for them.*

Step Four: *Finally, allow yourself to feel something new emerge: a new potential or possibility now that you have enlarged your perspective.*

Repeat this exercise for resentments you might have about yourself. Go through all four steps to notice how you might be thinking about your loved ones in ways that lead to some of your discomforts with them. Gradually you will be able to better sort out what might need to be changed on your part or on theirs.

Exercise 15.6: Forgive through Recognition of Suffering

When people are depressed, they often carry long-standing resentments. But holding on to resentments not only hurts the quality of relationships, it also hurts people emotionally. Learning to feel gratitude for the positive qualities in oneself and others can have a healing effect. Meditation offers ways to foster gratitude. Meditation can also help your clients to cultivate letting go of resentments through compassion, even in situations where real wrongdoing has occurred. Deliberate practice will bring results. Learning to forgive without taking offense, to have compassion for the plight of others, and even taking some transgressions lightly, will bring greater peace of mind. Reactions will change, and clients may even reach out to help others with positive effect. Open focus on compassion can help people to forgive.

Meditate on how the person you resent might be suffering. This person's irritating interactions may be an expression of discomforts he or she feels within. You can imagine the pain he or she may have. You might even know something about what this person has suffered in life. Let your mind wander around these topics and other associated ones. Understanding what it feels like to suffer as you have, you can feel compassion for someone else's suffering. You can use the depth of insight you have gained from examining, rethinking, and coping with your moods to recognize that others might suffer too. Thus, your own discomfort can serve a positive role, as your teacher, so you can in turn help others.

Exercise 15.7: Develop Gratitude

Depressed people are so focused on the negative that they often miss all the goodness around them. It might be a subtle moment, such as a beautiful bird flying by, or a true kindness extended by family or friends that is not perceived. The practice of gratitude can open perception to include more. As we discussed in Chapter 11, research has found that the practice of gratitude can help lift depression. Use the exercises in Chapter 11 as you help your client focus on gratitude. We have found these practices especially helpful for depressed clients and encourage you to work gently with your clients toward developing their capacity to appreciate the goodness that is also part of their lives.

You may not feel grateful as you begin, but allow your perception to move around the office now. Can you see anything that you might feel grateful for in the office? Perhaps it's a pillow that you like to lean on, a picture on the wall that you enjoy, or maybe the warm presence of your therapist. Now, can you expand that perception to include the environment outside the office? Is there anything that you feel grateful for? Perhaps you feel grateful for a store that has a particular item you buy regularly or maybe a person who is nice to you. Now, moving outward to your friends and family, can you think of any small thing you might appreciate about someone in your life? Even people who are difficult to deal with have fleeting moments when they might be kind or helpful. Allow yourself to look for the positive, even in places where it may seem hard to find. You may be pleasantly surprised to discover that there is much to be grateful for, and that in uncovering those moments, you feel better.

Exercise 15.8: Allow Well-Being

You can encourage your client to set the stage for feelings of well-being to emerge by meditating in a beautiful or comfortable place and allowing the natural response to occur. This is not an exercise in effort but rather an exercise in letting a natural response, with no specific focus, occur. Some people will respond immediately whereas others will feel a sense of well-being over time. Practice this meditation regularly to deepen the effects.

Allow yourself to meditate for a moment, perhaps out in nature or in a place where you feel comfortable. Sit quietly and look around. Enjoy the beauty you see and then let your mind clear of all thoughts. When a thought arises, notice it and then return to simply experiencing the surroundings and allowing soft, comfortable breathing. Sit this way for several minutes and allow the natural feelings of well-being to emerge, as they will when you practice in this way.

CONCLUSION

When people are depressed, their nervous system is underactivated, correlating with the feeling of lethargy and fatigue they often feel. Meditations to stimulate the nervous system can help depressed clients feel better. And mindfulness intervenes with the negative cognitive spiral of depression. As clients develop the ability to look at things without judgment and with acceptance, they will be able to respond more readily to psychotherapy as they work through the deeper issues. And by regular meditation practice, the brain grows new neural connections in key areas that counter the effects of depression and helps clients regulate their emotional responses better. In addition, the feelings of well-being that meditation elicits will bring a new sense of hope and joy that clients who are depressed so desperately seek. By adding meditation to your therapeutic work, you will enhance your outcomes as your depressed clients discover that they can find happiness and well-being.

16

Meditations for Bipolar Disorder

Core Principle 16: Use Meditation along with Medication to Rebalance the Nervous System, Strengthen Emotional Regulation, and Improve Relationships in Clients with Bipolar Disorder.

At the start of sneezing, during fright, in anxiety, above a chasm, flying in battle, in extreme curiosity, at the beginning of hunger, at the end of hunger, be uninterruptedly aware.

—From Vigyan Bhairav Tantra

INTRODUCTION

- Charting
- Mindfulness of daily habits
- Attuning to the call of your lifestyle
- Balancing energy with breathing meditations
- Enhancing relationships with focus meditations
- Turn awareness toward well-being

People who have bipolar disorder are often talented and creative individuals. In fact, those with bipolar disorder have been found to be more creative than the rest of the population (Murray & Johnson, 2010). Another unique set of qualities is the capacity, at times, to be perceptive, mentally sharp, and highly motivated. Often though, mood swings can make it harder for clients with bipolar disorder to truly actualize their potential, incorporating this. They can function with less awareness, out of touch with even the simple activities of eating, sleeping, and doing. The quote from the ancient Vigyan Bhairav Tantra suggests a sound method for those who suffer from bipolar disorder: meditative awareness. Meditation can help these clients tune in to their talents and creativity, making it easier for them to express their positive potentials as part of their everyday life.

Research reveals that people with bipolar disorder have structural abnormalities in neural pathways involved in regulating moods (Strakowski et al., 1999), including chronic overactivation in the amygdala and lower density in the cingulate gyrus. These brain imbalances that are associated with the swings in moods of bipolar disorder can be improved using medication. But medication is often not enough. Adding meditation to the client's daily routines can have a remarkably stabilizing effect on these brain areas as well as helping clients to feel more in control of their moods and energy.

The mental training that comes from practicing meditation increases activation in the cingulate gyrus while calming the amygdala. Regular meditation can increase interconnections between cortical regions and the limbic system to improve emotional regulation (Tang et al., 2009). In addition, meditation increases awareness in ways that can help clients with bipolar disorder help themselves to keep on track. These exciting findings offer compelling evidence that meditation can change brain patterns in clients with bipolar disorder and help them stabilize their moods and their lifestyle. Meditation can be used successfully in conjunction with medications and also for clients who are not using medications.

This chapter offers meditations for working with bipolar disorder. There is much clients with bipolar disorder can do in addition to taking medication, to keep steady and enhance their abilities. By becoming attuned to shifts in energy as they occur, these clients can prevent an episode before it begins. And with greater self-awareness, they will find it easier to develop a healthy and fulfilling lifestyle.

STABILIZING HABITS WITH AWARENESS

When they eat, they do not just eat, they conjure up all kinds of imagination; when they sleep, they do not just sleep, they are given up to varieties of idle thoughts, that is why theirs is not my way.

—D. T. Suzuki, The Zen Doctrine of No-Mind

We add disturbance and conflict to the simple activities of life. Meditation helps to clear all that away and get back to the activity itself. A Zen master once said, "When eating, just eat; when sleeping just sleep, when working just work. This is the secret of Zen." Clients with bipolar disorder will find balance and stability by engaging in their daily activities with awareness in this Zen way.

Bipolar disorder was originally labeled manic depression by Emil Kraepelin (1856–1926). After that term was shown to be incomplete, because the problem is more than simply static states of mania and melancholy, the name was changed. The disorder is best characterized as a cyclical flow of energy levels and moods, from low to high and back again, with periods of normality in between. Think of the disorder more like a sine wave of energy fluctuations. Mindfulness practice of simple daily routines can have a powerful effect by helping clients to notice these energy changes as they occur.

Begin by training mindfulness skills in therapy sessions. Then teach clients to practice mindfulness between sessions, noticing the flow of their energy as it occurs. There are outward signs, such as lessening of the appetite, quicker streams of thought, and reduced desire to sleep. Clients will begin to detect these subtle shifts as they are just beginning. This perception allows them to take appropriate actions to keep themselves stable.

The Man Who Attuned to the Waves of His Moods

A chemist who had been diagnosed with bipolar disorder came to see us to help with his moodiness. His psychiatrist was moving and had given him a referral for his medications, but he wanted to try to do more, so he asked us to help him. We encouraged him to try meditation. He began with short mindfulness practice in the office to learn the

(continued)

(*continued*)

skill. He liked the feeling of calm and balance and decided to use it when he surfed. He felt the rise and fall of the waves as he paddled out and experienced the push of the waves as he rode them into shore. We talked about the parallels to his mood swings, and he embraced the analogy. Just as he had attuned to the waves, he allowed himself to feel the pushes and pulls of his moods. He began to notice when he was heading into an upswing, how he felt less hungry and wanted less sleep. He became mindful of subtle cues, such as uptick in the speed of his thoughts, a loss of interest in food and sleep, and a shortening of his temper. And key to this process was his willingness to notice these changes mindfully. Then, just as he could steer the surfboard through the waves by moving his feet and altering his weight, he was able to make changes in his behavior by responding to mealtimes by eating and bedtime by sleeping. Gradually he steadied out, and his psychiatrist instructed him to lower his dose of medication.

Guide your clients toward making a commitment to establish stable positive routines. With your guidance and their own efforts to meditate, clients with bipolar disorder can bring balance to their life. The meditations that follow will help to enhance that process.

Exercise 16.1: The Daily Mood Chart to Initiate Awareness

Clients with bipolar disorder find themselves tossed and turned by the rolling seas of their shifting moods. They are often out of touch with their behaviors, such as eating and sleeping. We encourage charting of daily cycles to initiate a process of awareness by directing attention to their routines. Figure 16.1 is a chart clients can use to begin objectively observing their daily habits.

Mindful awareness gives a compass to steer by, to help attune to shifting energy levels for steady sailing. Through mindfulness practice and breathing meditations, clients can notice their mood shifts and intervene to keep themselves stabilized and attuned.

Fill out the chart below each day. You will find that by taking a moment to record different aspects of your day, you will initiate a process of self-awareness.

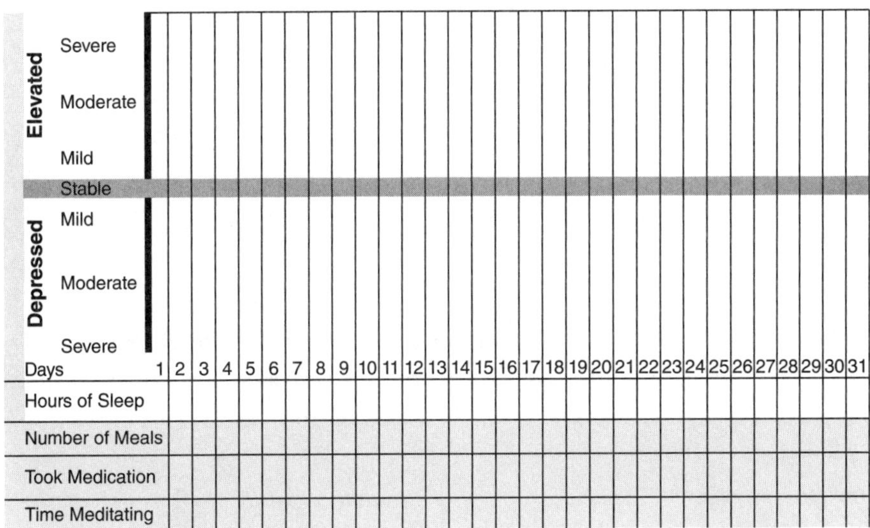

Figure 16.1   Daily Mood Chart

Exercise 16.2: Open Mindful Focus on Daily Routines

Review the mindfulness exercises in Chapter 9 and feel free to use any or all of them for this practice.

Be mindful of your experience at key points through the day. What do you notice as you wake up in the morning? Are you hungry for breakfast, or do you feel like skipping it? Be mindful of your emotions by observing what you are feeling. Notice your mental activity. What are you thinking or perceiving? Observe all these qualities quickly, as if scanning a horizon to take in everything all at once. You will notice a shift occurs as you become more centered in the here and now. You might be able to bring yourself to have a small breakfast even if you notice an urge to skip it.

Practice mindfulness just before your typical mealtimes, bedtimes, and waking times when you are stabilized. Stay aware as you notice what you are experiencing now. Keep noticing whatever you sense, feel, or think for several minutes. If your attention drifts, bring your attention back to mindful observing as soon as you can.

Exercise 16.3: Listening Mindfully to the Call of Your Lifestyle

Creating the lifestyle that will work for your client involves attuning to his or her deeper nature. Encourage your client to take mindful glances for one or two minutes at various times through the day. Integrating mindfulness into daily life helps to establish a more aware adjustment, in tune with deeper needs.

Perform mindfulness, noticing what you are experiencing at key times. Take note of patterns after careful, mindful attention to your experience. Then sense what you need. Perhaps you notice, as you pay attention, that you are feeling exhausted and overworked in the afternoon. Have you pushed yourself too hard all morning? Perhaps you need to add a 15-minute relaxation meditation into your afternoon schedule. Or maybe you perceive that you feel bored. You may not have included any time for meaningful work or creative efforts. Be attuned to what you need and want for your life, and be sure to make it part of your lifestyle.

The meditative way can guide you to what is fulfilling. You are inclined toward becoming complete: There is a tendency to seek balance, harmony of the center—homeostasis—which will begin to guide you if you listen to the subtle cues.

BALANCING ENERGY

Clients with bipolar disorder can learn to moderate their energy, keeping some of the positive enthusiasm of the mania or the quieter sensitivity from the depression without letting either go too far. Recall that meditation has a dual effect: It raises alertness and relaxation simultaneously. By calming the nervous system meditatively when it is over aroused, meditators remain alert and energetic. And by using meditation to raise energy when depressed (see Chapter 15), your clients will feel some relief and gain resources to work on disturbances. Moderating energy from both directions helps to be productive and direct motivation into meaningful endeavors.

Exercise 16.4: Focus on Breathing to Attune to Energy and Emotions

Attention to breathing can aid clients to sense energy levels intuitively. As you turn a client's attention to breathing at various times during the day, she may become aware of different qualities to her breathing. For example, when energy levels are beginning to rise, her breathing rate may be quicker with short breaths. By contrast, when she is feeling a downturn in mood, her breathing may be slower and shallow. By learning to notice the differences in all phases of the cycle and to accept them as expressions of inner being, your clients will attune meditatively to every moment.

Always start from where you are, without trying to change anything at first. As you sit patiently breathing now, awareness deepens and changes begin to happen of themselves. Remember that each moment is new, so even an uncomfortable breathing pattern will tend to alter. Take an inward glance at your breathing for a few minutes here and there throughout the day, and you will gain new intuitive understanding of the timing, pattern, and rhythm in the different moods of your cycles.

Exercise 16.5: Focus on the Calm Breath to Ease a Mood

Use your ability to calm your breathing whenever needed and you might feel an easing of a mood. When feeling a strong mood, turn your attention to your breathing. Now, begin with the breathing meditation from Chapter 8, "Bringing Attention from Outside to Inside," by placing your hands lightly on your lower rib cage and noticing how your hands move in and out with each breath. Then, when you feel attuned to breathing, let your attention move to awareness of each breath, as the air comes in and goes out. Take in each breath gently and breathe softly. Let each breath become softer and softer. Keep breathing in this way, with your attention focused just on breathing gently. After a time, you may find that your mood eases slightly in response to your change in breathing.

Exercise 16.6: Focus on Balancing the Breath

This exercise balances energy between the two sides of the body while also enhancing concentration. Refer to the instructions for Nostril Breathing and Figures 7.4 and Figure 7.5 in Chapter 7. Begin by practicing for several minutes, and increase the time to 30 minutes each day. If you have trouble staying focused, you can do this exercise for short periods, two to three minutes, several times each day. The key when doing the exercise for a brief period is to do it often. With either timing approach, you will find a noticeable shift in energy and emotions toward a more calm and centered experience.

ENHANCING AWARENESS OF OTHERS

You may have noticed that your clients with bipolar disorder have problems in their interpersonal relationships, especially during an up- or a down-swing. Research has shown that persons with bipolar disorder have difficulty recognizing emotions in facial expressions of others. One study showed that people with bipolar I , the most extreme form of bipolar disorder, had significantly lower emotional recognition than did subjects with bipolar II disorder and normal subjects (Derntl, Seidel, Kryspin-Exner, Hasmann, & Dobmeier, 2009). Another study found the same impairment perception of facial emotions in subjects with mania (Lembke & Ketter, 2002). Depressed subjects had difficulty recognizing fear and disgust but were able to recognize the other emotions accurately. These deficits relate to the changes in the brain that occur with bipolar disorder. As a result, clients with bipolar disorder may misperceive the feelings of others, including feelings directed toward them. Misunderstandings may arise that complicate their interpersonal relationships. Meditative awareness can help clients with bipolar disorder to improve their accuracy in recognizing the emotions of others.

Exercise 16.7: Focus Meditation on Other's Facial Expression

Practice manifesting an emotion, and have your client observe carefully and then tell you what emotion you are expressing. With mindful attention combined with accurate feedback, your clients can improve their ability to realistically recognize emotions in others.

Turn your attention to your therapist's face. Notice all the details mindfully. Then guess what emotion you think is being expressed. Once you have guessed correctly, focus again, thinking about the emotion being expressed while you look. Go through the four primary emotions: happiness, sadness, anger, and fear.

If possible, perform this exercise between sessions with several different people. Tell the other person what emotion you perceive them expressing. Ask the other person to give you feedback on your guesses about their emotions. By carefully focusing your attention combined with receiving feedback as to whether you are correct or not, you will improve in your ability to recognize emotions in others.

Exercise 16.8: Focus Meditation on Listening

People are accustomed to thinking about the meaning of what people are saying, but they rarely pay attention to the sound of their own voice. Voice tones express emotional meaning as well as facial expressions, adding emotional information. Help your client enhance the ability to relate well to others by turning their mindful attention to the sound of the voice.

Focus your attention on the sounds and voice tones as you speak. Rather than concentrating on what you are trying to say, turn your attention to the sound of your voice as you speak. Hear the tones, the pitch, and the volume. Do your words come out quickly or slowly? Do you speak with expression or is your speech flat and unemotional? Pay attention to the quality of speech. By doing so, you may begin to attune to your deeper thoughts and feelings.

Next, focus your attention on the other person's voice tones in conversation. Extend this meditation to listen when the other speaks as he or she is feeling each of the primary emotions. Listen to others as they speak to you in many situations. You may be surprised by how much information is conveyed by the tone of the voice, not just the words.

FOSTERING WELL-BEING

Clients with bipolar disorder will benefit by some positive psychology input that helps them accept themselves in a realistic way. Typically creative, these clients likely have some undeveloped talents wanting to be expressed. Nurture self-acceptance and the use of their meditative skills to keep them attuned. In time, they will get in touch with their true abilities. Help them channel their talents by getting the training they need or making time for self-expression, either as a hobby or as part of their work. And encourage them to have faith in their strong, capable nature, filled with potential. Even though this nature may be obscured at times by the dark shadows of their moods, like the sun hidden behind the clouds, it is always there.

Exercise 16.9: No-Focus Trust of Your Deeper Nature Meditation

Sit quietly and allow your breathing to settle. Quiet your thoughts as you let them flow. Trust your deeper nature here and now as you just sit quietly and sense.

Don't think about anything in particular as you relax very deeply. Feel your oneness with everything around you, part of the flow of your life. Be without thought, in this moment, free and at peace. The winds of your energies are flowing within you. Accept what you sense as you sit calmly now. May the hidden light of your awareness brighten your way, bringing happiness and fulfillment.

CONCLUSION

Encourage your clients to turn to meditation regularly, even if only for a moment throughout the day. As they attune to their flow of energy meditatively, their mindful attention and your encouragement toward balance can guide them to find stability for their lives. From a more stable, balanced lifestyle and mood, your bipolar clients will be more capable of creatively expressing their unique nature and finding fulfillment.

17

Meditations for Anxiety

Core Principle 17: Counter the Negative Anticipation toward the Future Found in Anxiety Disorders. Center the Client in the Present Moment.

Focusing on your present moment experience goes beyond simply trying to find pleasure. The practice of being engaged, focused, and present is in itself a steadying and soothing sensation.

—Donald Altman, The Mindfulness Toolbox

INTRODUCTION

- Bring attention to the present moment.
- Calm the nervous system.
- Deconstruct anxiety sensations.
- Become mindful in everyday life.

Meditation's moment-by-moment awareness brings people into the present. This experience, in and of itself, has a healing effect. People suffering from anxiety are often caught in uncomfortable anticipation of a negative future. The gap they feel between experiencing now and expecting what will be experienced later is diminished as the meditator stays with each experience, moment to moment. When attention is used in this way, there is no anticipation of the future. And since evaluative awareness is discouraged, negative judgments are suspended as well, so that the discomforts can be experienced as just sensations and nothing more. This helps to ease worries and dread, bringing the nervous system back into balance.

Meditation research shows a dual effect of calm with alertness, as we described in Chapter 3. Regular meditation practice brings about a measurable reduction in tension, anxiety, stress, and emotional disturbance. The dual effect of calm combined with alertness will help your clients experience a lowering of their anxiety. In addition, the meditative techniques can serve as correctives for clients' faulty thought patterns and overactivated emotional responses.

HOW ANXIETY CHANGES THE MIND AND BRAIN

Anxiety is a mind-body problem. People who suffer from anxiety have uncomfortable body sensations while also experiencing worried thoughts. They often know that they shouldn't feel so anxious but feel helpless to change the reaction. The many brain systems that are involved help to explain anxiety reactions.

During an anxiety reaction, the amygdala, the gateway to the limbic system, is activated and sends a signal to the hypothalamus that there is something wrong. The hypothalamus, as the coordinator of internal functions, activates the hypothalamic-pituitary-adrenal (HPA) fear/stress pathway, which puts the autonomic nervous system on high alert. The hippocampus, where memories are processed and integrated, adds to the signal. In addition, the insula, which registers internal sensations, is activated by the inner discomforts. These bodily pains are interpreted with dread, as if something bad is coming. The cortex gets involved, generating disturbing thoughts and ruminations about the state of affairs. The anxious person is looking toward the future, with signals from the body and mind forecasting impending disaster. But when the person has been anxious over time, the HPA activation becomes chronic and brain tissue adapts. Normal connectivity between the amygdala and frontal, occipital, and temporal lobes is decreased, making it difficult for clients with anxiety to regulate and to quell their worries.

Clients who meditate regularly can lower their anxiety levels. The practice of meditation brings a calmer adjustment. And the alertness clients develop will help them to be more responsive to your interventions. The meditations that follow are designed specifically to help develop the skill of alert calm.

STAY IN THE PRESENT MOMENT

Mindfulness brings the client back to the present moment. When practicing mindfulness, guide the client to make special note of how each sensation is a new one, with new potential for adapting. Deliberate cultivation of this attitude helps to neutralize anxious anticipation.

Breathing is a gateway to experience. By relaxing the breath, clients can bring about greater calm all over. You can use any of the breathing meditations in this book, but for anxiety, we have found that combining breathing meditation with movement may be easier for clients.

Exercise 17.1: Open-Focus Mindfulness: Breathing in the Present Moment

Start with breathing. Notice that each breath is a new and different breath. Even though the last breath resembles the next one, it is not the same breath. Everything is slightly different with each new moment. With the felt understanding of how each breath is unique, consider that each anxiety attack is unique too. Every time the anxiety occurs is a new time, a little different from the last one. Even though the experience seems to be exactly like the last time, it actually is unique and new. People often compress all their anxious experiences together into one dreaded experience. Follow each moment anew, to discover how each moment offers a new opportunity to let the anxiety go. Relax as much as possible with each breath.

CALM THE NERVOUS SYSTEM

Unfortunately, some anxious clients find that trying to sit quietly to meditate makes them feel more anxious. In these cases, you can add some movement to meditation. The quality of mind, alert, calm, and focused, is what you are trying to bring about. Meditation on movement can bring about this alert and focused attention while also remaining calm.

Exercise 17.2: Focused Awareness on Movement

Sit comfortably for a moment. Then lift your arms very slowly, with palms up, as you pay close attention to the movement. Notice the sensation in your arms, your palms, and your fingers as you gradually raise your arms to shoulder height. Keep your attention fully focused on moving and nothing else. If your attention drifts away, gently bring it back to the movement as soon as you notice. Then, moving just as slowly, turn your palms over and lower your arms slowly until they rest on your lap. Pay attention to your arms now at rest for a minute or two and then repeat.

Exercise 17.3: Focused Awareness of Movement with the Breath

Now let yourself correlate breathing with movement. Stand comfortably and breathe naturally for a moment or two. Then, when you feel centered in your experience, gently raise your arms as you did in the "Mindful with Movement" meditation earlier in this chapter, only with a difference. This time, time your movement to match your breathing. So, as you inhale, raise your arms; then, as you exhale, slowly lower them. Don't change your breathing. Coordinate each inhale with raising and each exhale with lowering. Continue in this way, breathing gently and moving slowly together. Keep your attention focused on breathing and moving. When you are finished, stand for a moment with your arms comfortably at your sides and experience the sensations. Do you feel tingling or warmth in your arms? Notice whatever you feel. You may find that you feel a pleasant calm now.

Exercise 17.4: Focused Attention for Releasing Chronic Tension

Anxious clients often carry chronic tensions. Sometimes clients tense up when they don't really need to, wasting energy and exhausting their resources. It is possible to notice when radiating extra tension and let go of it by learning to take an occasional meditative glance during activity. It can be done quickly and subtly. As your clients learn to carry less unnecessary tension with them through the day, they will begin to form a basis for a more regulated, aware life.

Turn your attention inward. Are you tightening up unnecessarily? Notice your body sensations. Is your jaw clenched? Are your shoulders raised? Is your back hunched? Is your stomach tense? Do you feel tightness in your legs and arms? If you find that you are tense, ask yourself whether you need that tension. Whenever you notice tension that you don't need, try to let go of it gently. You will find times when you can allow yourself to be more relaxed in your daily life. Perform this meditation when you are in these situations. Can you allow some increased relaxation? An inward glance helps you open the possibility if you discover that you could become more relaxed.

Exercise 17.5: Guided Meditation: Focusing on a Calm Image

For clients who respond well to structure in therapy, you may want to use a guided imagery meditation to keep them focused toward calmness. They can use this image (or any other that may be more individually attuned to their lives) between sessions to elicit a calming effect.

Perform this exercise with your eyes closed. During this visualization, your eyes will relax, along with your mind. Have you ever enjoyed the experience of skipping stones over the water? To do so, you must find a very flat stone and throw it sideways, so that it just touches the water and bounces off repeatedly. With practice, you may be able to skip the stone seven, eight, or more times. Even if you haven't actually done it yourself, you can probably imagine it. Visualize a calm body of water, such as a lake. Take a few moments to look around you. Do large trees surround the lake? Is there a sandy beach? Can you smell the clean air? Feel a gentle breeze? Imagine that you or someone else steps up to the shore to skip stones. Picture the stone as it skips out along the surface of the water. Imagine that it skips a number of times. Picture it as vividly as you can. As you watch the stone skim along the lake, you might find your body and mind relaxes comfortably.

DECONSTRUCT ANXIETY SENSATIONS

Anxiety sometimes involves linking uncomfortable body sensations in the chest to beliefs about what such physical symptoms usually signify, to worry about having a heart attack, expectations about that possibility, and so on. A real and existing pattern emerges from associating these components together, although not originally from an actual heart condition. Even if a medical checkup determines that there is no underlying physical cause, to become free from the anxiety, the sufferer still must believe and accept that there is actually nothing there. The following Story illustrates how to deconstruct this pattern of mental construction.

The Man Who Learned to Accept His Sensations

A medical practitioner came for treatment because of anxiety. Often when seeing his patients, he felt such intense anxiety that he had to leave the room. This problem was interfering with his work. He worried that he was dying and could not dispel his anxiety. He went to his doctor complaining that he was having a heart attack. His doctor told him that no, he didn't have a heart condition. What was wrong was that his rib cage tended to constrict at his solar plexus, giving him sensations of difficulty when he breathed. As his body aged, his rib cage became less flexible. Now in his 40s, the man experienced the sensations as severe and sharp. His doctor told him, "I can fix this problem. I will refer you to a surgeon I know, and he will break all your ribs and re-form them so that you will have more room for breathing." Our client thought to himself, "I think I will try something else." And so he came to us and said, "Can you help me?"

We taught him meditation and hypnosis, and he learned to become calm in the sessions but still felt anxiety during the week. Gradually, as he improved his meditation skills, we taught him how to mindfully recognize his sensation and experience it as simply that, a feeling of comfort or discomfort. The interpretation he had been giving it—a possible heart attack or serious problem—was a further alarming evaluation that he made. He had checked with his medical doctor and knew that he was not in danger of a heart attack. He learned to distinguish when he was evaluating a sensation (This feels awful) from simply noticing its quality and intensity. He learned to be more neutral as he observed carefully, without making any negative evaluations. In time, the discomfort lessened. He continued to practice mindfulness at work and at home, so that whenever he felt the anxiety, he could notice it mindfully and watch it diminish. Eventually, he worked through some issues that were fueling his anxious reactions, and the symptoms went away completely.

Exercise 17.6: Deconstruction Meditation for Anxiety with Open-Focus Mindfulness

Meditation can be applied to relieve anxiety when medical exams have shown that there is nothing wrong. The first step is to contemplate the idea that sensation and cognition can be separated. A pure sensation and the thoughts about the sensation can be distinguished, and this helps manage the situation. Review the different forms of mindfulness: of body, of emotions, of mind, and of objects of mind. Refer to the mindfulness instructions in Chapter 9, and practice these meditations when your clients are not feeling anxious. As skills build, it becomes possible to maintain mindfulness even while feeling tense, especially if clients are already familiar with the meditation.

Mentally break down the anxiety into its component parts. Anxiety can be thought of as a conglomerate of moments during which a frightening interpretation is added to describe an uncomfortable sensation. This process tends to increase the intensity of the sensation, leading to a further interpretation, such as "It's getting worse." Each successive moment includes an interpretation followed by an even stronger sensation in reaction. First, observe this spiraling process as it unfolds. Then, as soon as possible, notice the separate parts: sensations, interpretations, and emotions. Try to recognize that the interpretations are separate from and are not the same as the sensations or the emotions.

Now extend the meditation. Notice how the components influence and are inseparably part of each other: Worrying interpretations provoke more worry. And the worry brings on more discomfort, in a self-perpetuating cycle. Question the realistic certainty of this reaction with inwardly focused reassurance, such as: "I know that my worry may not necessarily be what the sensation will bring; I have checked out my condition and I know that there is no physical problem."

Be patient with the process. Remember that time is a limiting factor. Recall a past anxiety attack when the discomfort passed after a certain amount of time. Remember that even when expecting that the feeling might be a sign of terrible things, when nothing happened, the anxiety sensations eventually passed anyway. It is important to recognize that there is a difference between reacting to what is actually taking place and reacting to what you expect will take place, in a possible future.

Keep returning to staying in each moment as it comes rather than anticipating what it might become. Allow breathing to find a natural rhythm appropriate to the moment. Try to carefully follow experiencing mindfully as it happens, including the periods of time that the feeling diminishes. Anxiety in general tends to become easier to handle and eventually lessens in intensity.

HOW TO MEDITATE BETWEEN SESSIONS

To alter a long-standing anxiety pattern, people will need to meditate between sessions to bring about a change in mind and body. Encourage your clients to meditate between sessions, using any of the meditations in this book. Encourage them to begin with the meditations they like best.

When you suggest that your client meditate between sessions, you might get this response: "I'm too busy! I don't have time to meditate!" Make it easier for your clients to find time to meditate by suggesting that they start with one-minute meditations, but perform these one-minute meditations several times each day. Encourage them to increase the time gradually when they feel ready.

Exercise 17.7: Warm-up with Meditation on a Very Brief Activity

Encourage clients who have difficulty sustaining meditation for very long to pick a short activity that they perform every day. Many activities can be used for this. Every moment is an opportunity to become more aware, so busy clients can meditate in many different situations. One example is brushing the teeth.

Often anxious clients lack awareness of what they are doing as they do it. Some are overly concerned with inner turmoil that keeps their attention away from the world. Others filter their experience through the distorted lens of their disturbed past or live in a difficult environment with unsatisfying relationships. Your clients will benefit from sharpening their perception to become attuned to their everyday lives in a realistic way. When people fully attend to what they do while they do it, they will experience the circumstances of their lives differently, often becoming more accepting and less troubled. This is a useful exercise to assign as homework between sessions.

Decide to attend to the task mindfully, from beginning to end. Before beginning, stop for a few seconds and breathe with awareness of each breath in and out. Then begin the activity: Notice the taste of the toothpaste, the temperature of the water, and the sensation of the toothbrush on the teeth. Feel your arm as it moves, and notice your body position at the sink. Notice what you are thinking as you brush. If you find yourself making a judgment—"I feel anxious," "I don't like this feeling"—notice that you are doing so, but set the judgment aside and return to your direct experience. When finished, take a few seconds to pay attention to the sensation of your mouth and face.

Exercise 17.8: Meditation on an Activity

In this meditation, you can bring your meditative presence to the activities of your everyday life. Choose something simple that you usually rush through without paying too much attention, because you think of it as a mundane chore. One possibility is washing the dishes or washing the car. Any activity of this kind can become an opportunity to contemplate.

Before you begin, close your eyes. Clear your mind of thoughts, then sense your body. If you are standing by the sink or beside your car, notice all the details of your experience. Are your arms tense or relaxed in preparation? How do you feel as you are about to engage in washing? Now begin the activity. Feel the sudsy water as you wash. Smell the soap. Watch the dirt as it slides off the surface. Watch the patterns. Listen to the sounds. Notice the aesthetic qualities of your experience and allow yourself to be interested in what you are doing as you do it. When you have finished, close your eyes once more and clear your mind again. Then open your eyes. How do you feel now?

Perform this meditation with many kinds of tasks that are part of your day, but do so one at a time at first. As you advance, practice with your regular daily activities, concentrating on each action of a sequence as you do it. If your mind spontaneously wanders by inattention or otherwise resists, do not worry about it.

Accept it, include it as in the clearing mind exercises, and continue to practice. Relax enough to release unnecessary tensions but not so much as to be unaware or inefficient. You can extend this general attitude into almost any realm of action.

Exercise 17.9: No-Focus Quiet Sitting

Often people drive themselves to be busy. But how often do we allow ourselves to simply sit quietly, with nothing in mind? Neuroscience has found that even when we are quietly doing nothing, the brain is still active. A default mode network of the brain is activated, a kind of set point for restful being. Anxiety can be relieved by quiet sitting, which allows the nervous system to refresh and the mind to be at ease. Paradoxically, just sitting quietly and allowing the mind to wander returns control, just as steering in the direction that wheels are skidding on ice while carefully reducing speed will return control of the car to the driver, until it is tracking correctly on the road.

Take a moment for quiet sitting with nothing in mind. Just sit comfortably for several minutes, and allow your mind to be free. Don't think about anything, simply let yourself be quiet and at ease. If you find yourself planning for the future or ruminating about the past, gently bring your mind back to simply sitting. Do this from time to time. You may find it restful and renewing—an oasis in the midst of a busy day.

CONCLUSION

Regular meditation is helpful for changing an anxiety pattern. If your clients can't sustain a long meditation, encourage a number of short sessions each day. Add movement if your clients have trouble sitting still. And include regular calming along with mindfulness throughout the day. Anxiety responds well to meditative therapy. Your clients will feel a tremendous relief and sense of well-being as they rewire their brains for better regulation and calmer adjustment.

18

Meditations for Trauma

Core Principle 18: Train the Mind and Brain after Trauma to Elicit Calm, Build Resilience, and Rediscover Well-being.

Meditation's calm
Sweet incense it brings
Restores peaceful inner wellsprings
Helping to shed all cares,
Soothes the soul
Clears the mind
Makes you whole.

—C. Alexander Simpkins

INTRODUCTION

- Create an experience of safety and security wherever you are.

- Mindfully observe trauma triggers, emotions, thoughts, and behaviors.

- Reconsolidate traumatic memories from your sanctuary for lasting change.
- Nurture self-support and self-acceptance.
- Develop compassion and forgiveness.

Clients who have experienced trauma have been through an intensely threatening, dangerous, life-threatening experience involving themselves or someone else. And yet, even though exposure to trauma often has harmful effects, it can also stimulate resilience, toughness, and meaningful change. Researchers have found that moderate amounts of adversity might enable people to handle future stressors better (Meichenbaum, 2012). Thus, the trauma provides an opportunity for your client to grow stronger. Meditation provides practices that not only help clients recover from debilitating trauma but also provide an opportunity to transform trauma into growth.

HOW TRAUMA CHANGES THE MIND, BRAIN, AND BODY

The body has an unconscious system that helps us to detect a threat, a brain-body response at the level of the nervous system. Several brain systems with a link to cognitions and emotions are involved. When facing a perceived threat, the amygdala sends messages to your endocrine system as part of the HPA fear/stress pathway that links the hypothalamus, pituitary, and adrenal glands together. The HPA pathway is not only activated by an immediate threat; it is also triggered by memories of the trauma. Memories are stored in the hippocampus, located right next to the amygdala. This close proximity leads to a strong interaction between the hippocampus and amygdala, helping to explain how many trauma sufferers keep remembering the threat even though it occurred in the past.

Even though many trauma sufferers are haunted by traumatic memories day and night, others do not consciously remember traumatic memories. Memory has two main systems, one explicit and conscious, and the other implicit and unconscious. Explicit memory includes memorizing facts (semantic memory), such as the name of your country's leader or the date of a certain holiday. Explicit memory also includes remembering events that are part of your personal life (episodic memory), such as what you had for breakfast or how you celebrated your last birthday. These forms of memory work through the higher-level prefrontal cortex and the hippocampus.

Memory of a trauma is influenced by the release of cortisol during the traumatic experience. The explicit memory system may be blocked by too much or too little cortisol, which helps to explain why some clients have little or no memory of the traumatic event while others cannot forget. Often when people have trauma as adults, as from war experiences, rape, and natural disasters, the memories are intensely disturbing and keep recurring. When trauma is acquired in early childhood, the infant or very young child may not be able to process the experience consciously. These memories become implicit, which means unconscious. They are stored in the amygdala, never going through the hippocampus to be consolidated into consciousness. Thus, some of your clients may have uncomfortable feelings without any conscious memory of the event itself while others continually relive the trauma.

Treatment for trauma involves helping clients to reconsolidate the traumatic memory, either consciously or unconsciously, so that they will see it in a new way and ease their overreactive nervous system. The memory can literally transform, being remapped in the brain in a new way through neuroplasticity, bringing about posttraumatic growth. Meditation can also help to rebalance the nervous system to a healthier, less stressed level. And clients can mobilize their strengths to develop resilience to meet future challenges well.

FINDING SECURITY

When people have suffered trauma, they carry a sense of danger with them. They see the world as an unsafe place, finding threat lurking everywhere. The story of our client, Triana, provides an example of how an early trauma, stored implicitly, can lead to unexplained anxiety later in life.

The Woman Who Unlocked the Key to Her Trauma

Triana was a competent woman. She had worked with an older man as a newscaster on television and was a rising star. But she suffered from panic attacks and felt compelled to resign from her on-camera job to work as a behind-the-scenes reporter. She missed the excitement of the nightly newscast, so she asked us to help her get back to the work she

(continued)

(continued)

loved. We offered a combination of hypnosis with meditation. She told us that when she was very young, her parents had divorced, and she lived with her mother. During one session, a surprising implicit memory emerged. Triana remembered a time when her grandparents came for a visit. She was quite young, around three-years old, and snuck down the stairs to listen to them in the kitchen, talking about her father. "He's a rat," shouted her grandfather. "You can't trust him after he the way he hurt that child!" Triana knew they were talking about her. Although she had no memory of the event, nor did she remember her father, she always carried a nervous, unsafe feeling around men and hadn't realized it. As she recalled the memory, she cried deeply, She re-experienced the pain and suffering she hadn't felt since she was a child. We guided her to accept her feelings as she felt them now, in the sanctuary of our office. We encouraged her to recognize that she was a grown woman now, with many resources. She took some deep breaths, allowed herself to feel mindfully in the present moment. Over time, meditation helped her to stay grounded in her present experience, to accept that she was okay now, and let go of the hurts from the past.

Meditation develops a calm center, a sense of being safe and secure. Meditation, which is not dependent on anything outside of the client's own resources, can bring that refuge that trauma sufferers so desperately seek.

Ultimately, life is always changing. There is no enduring external security. The best source for safety and security is found by grounding in awareness. Meditation offers methods for developing a personal sense of security, drawing on the wellsprings within.

Exercise 18.1: Meditative Focus on Sanctuary

Clients can enlist their own experiences from the past to visualize a safe place and go there imaginatively as a resource. When we present this meditation, we ask clients to think of a time when they felt calm, secure, and comfortable. Usually people think of a tranquil place in nature, but it might be a memory of feeling cozy at home or with someone special. You can also give your clients a peaceful image to visualize. We offer a peaceful scene here of being near the ocean, but feel free to invite clients to find their own sanctuary if they prefer.

You are sitting on the sand at a beach late in the afternoon. The sand feels warm as the sun shines with just a few fluffy white clouds. The sea breeze is cool and refreshing on your skin. You can smell the fresh salt air as you take a deep breath in and relax. The waves are coming in regular, perfectly formed sets. You can hear the wave break along the shore, a soothing sound that fills your consciousness with nature's wonder. Some time passes as you feel completely relaxed, and the sun begins to set over the ocean. Gradually rich red and orange streaks stretch across the sky. As the sun lowers, the colors intensify and deepen. The bright yellow-orange sun sinks behind the horizon, and as it finally goes, you see a green flash. Now the sky turns purple-red, and you feel awed by the majestic beauty all around you. Every sunset is unique, and you can always return to this place and enjoy the calm beauty of the ocean.

Exercise 18.2: No-Focus Clearing Away Disturbance to Find Inner Peace

Meditation can give sanctuary based on a here-and-now moment of presence, without need for thought. You can carry peace of mind with you always and anywhere. The true source of harmony is within, and letting go of thought lets it begin.

Sit quietly in meditation. Let all your sensations settle. Breathe comfortably, in and out, allowing your breathing rate to be relaxed and calm. Now let your mind clear of all thought. As soon as a new thought appears, let it go and return to meditating without thought. Keep working on letting your stream of consciousness be clear of thought. In that moment of "no-thought," there is no worry or stress. Everything is serene and peaceful. Here is true sanctuary, always available if you simply make the effort to recognize that it is there.

WORKING THROUGH TRAUMATIC MEMORIES

You can initiate a change in clients' trauma patterns and literally help them to rewire the brain so that the reaction will no longer be the same. The next series of exercises takes you through a process of becoming mindfully aware of the pattern and changing the pattern with several different meditations so that the memory is reconsolidated in a new way. Sometimes trauma memory work may not require making the traumatic events explicit. But we begin with an approach to transform unconscious and conscious traumatic experiences. Use some of the stress exercises in Chapter 13 for shifting the nervous system back into balance, and refer to the anxiety and substance abuse Chapters 17 and 19 for additional exercises to guide in working with the trauma through body meditations, for nonconscious change.

Although the memory of trauma is often implicit, any related experiences or events might trigger a reaction. This reaction sets in motion an automatic set of emotions, thoughts, and behaviors that gathers momentum. Mindfulness can help clients become aware of the trauma in the safe, nonthreatening situation with you in the office. This new context for re-experiencing alters the past memory, helping clients find new meaning and allowing them to move forward to a better future.

Exercise 18.3: Open-Focus Mindfulness on Triggers

Perform mindfulness in the sanctuary of the office, where your clients can feel safe and protected. Your therapeutic presence can be reassuring and allow them to feel more comfortable when they enter the dark territory of trauma. Practice this mindfulness meditation soon after the moment when an emotional reaction has been triggered, perhaps after bringing up some memories. Use your therapeutic judgment by not pushing the client to handle too much discomfort. So, you might practice this exercise for a few minutes, then ask the client to relax and breathe calmly with you for a few minutes, and then when ready, return to being mindful.

Stop and pay attention to what you are experiencing. Suspend judgment, simply observe, and trust that mindful awareness will be helpful. As soon as you react, notice your emotions. What do you feel? Observe your sensations (e.g., heart beating rapidly, palms sweating, stomach tightening) as well as your feelings (e.g., panic, frightened, angry) and any other experiences you might be having. Trust that this is a healing process.

Do you notice any thought patterns that arise? What are you saying to yourself inwardly? If you observe negativity, notice how your thinking unfolds. Do your thoughts become increasingly negative? Do you get into an internal argument? Do your thoughts repeat, or are you thinking a long, escalating series of thoughts? Notice how you are thinking these thoughts in the present moment, safe here in the office.

Now turn your attention to your behavior. What do you feel like doing as you feel and think? Do you want to withdraw and keep to yourself? Perhaps you feel like exploding with anger. Or maybe you find your eyes tearing. How does your body respond? Perhaps it tightens up or just feels fatigued. As always, observe nonjudgmentally. Then look around the room and become aware of the present moment in your therapy session. An inner dialogue about what you observe may help. The patterns of your body sensations give clues to deeper emotional and cognitive meanings, but they may not easily be made explicit or rational.

Remain mindful without judgment whenever the negative experience arises. Keep working on letting evaluations go. Although there may be much truth in the fact that the event was terrible, negative judgments don't help to reduce the effects. Instead, keep returning to awareness of the present moment, focusing on here and now. By accepting what is going on in the present, you open the way to reconsolidate the traumatic memory in a new way so that it is no longer troubling.

Exercise 18.4: Open-Focus Mindful Reconsolidating of Traumatic Memories from a Safe Place

Return to your sanctuary place, or simply become mindfully aware of the office now where you feel safe and secure. Allow comfortable calm to develop. Now recall the emotions, thoughts, and behaviors you are working on. Feel them for a few minutes, and notice mindfully what you experience from your safe place. Take the support that is there for you. How does your experience change? Perhaps the emotions diminish, or maybe you feel stronger or more support from others. Mindful in the present moment, you can feel your emotions while maintaining a mindful, observing calm. Through this process, the memory is altered. You may need to repeat this exercise a number of times to make the discoveries you need.

NURTURE SELF-ACCEPTANCE AND COMPASSION

The experience your clients have while meditating brings a sense that they are the master of their life. They may not be able to control contingency, but they can control how they interpret it. People can be strong even when they have experienced a traumatic event, by cultivating acceptance and resiliency meditatively. They will be able to accept themselves more fully when they can forgive, not only the perpetrator, but also forgive themselves. Then they will be able to accept compassion from others and from themselves, a key to healing trauma.

Exercise 18.5: Accept Yourself Right Now

Meditate on breathing for a few minutes, noticing each breath, in and out. Your breathing finds its own natural rhythm. All you have to do is allow it to happen. Many things in our physiology are like this. When you have the flu, you can drink extra water and get sufficient rest, but, ultimately, nature takes its course. The immune system of your body takes care of it, and your body eventually heals. Similarly, with trauma, if you take care of your physical and psychological health, your brain-mind-body system will find its natural balance again. Nature will take its course. Are there other examples of how the mind-brain-body system can restore balance of itself? As you sit in meditation now, can you accept yourself as you are now? Trust that you can return to normal when the time is right, allowing your recovery process to take the time it needs. Our brains are capable of neuroplasticity and neurogenesis, to grow and develop as needed. Have confidence in the process.

Exercise 18.6: Develop Compassion and Forgiveness

Learning to forgive is difficult for many clients, but it is an important part of trauma recovery, especially when someone has done something harmful and hurtful. Practicing compassion exercises that extend feelings of understanding for the other shows clients how their resentment and anger only perpetuates their own pain. This exercise can help people extend their own feelings of compassion not just to others but also to themselves. Repeat this exercise and Exercise 18.5 on acceptance often. Over time, your client will be able to make the transition from a person who feels unworthy and unacceptable to one who feels her/his self-worth and self-acceptance.

Think about the person you are angry with and resent. Can you imagine the suffering this person has experienced to shape his or her actions? Just as you would feel compassion for a suffering animal that might lash out, can you extend your compassion and even forgiveness to this person who has hurt you, recognizing that this person is suffering in his or her way too. As you let go of your resentment and extend your compassion, allow your own body to relax.

Now, can you extend that compassion and forgiveness to yourself as well? This might involve forgiving yourself for things you may have done that you believe were wrong or bad. Can you recognize that under the difficult circumstances you faced, you did what you felt you had to do? Forgive yourself now, recognize that you are much more than those negative past experiences. People often feel their compassion in the heart area. Allow. Trust yourself now, in the present moment as you allow the feelings of compassion to spread through you.

CONCLUSION

Trauma involves disturbing memories that can be conscious or unconscious. Meditation provides ways to create the calm and inner strength needed to overcome these overwhelming experiences and come out the other side stronger and wiser. Encourage regular meditation practice to enhance the effects and to serve as a reliable resource for the future.

19

Meditations for Substance Abuse

Core Principle 19: Rewire the Reward Pathway
of the Brain to Go beyond Pleasure and Pain and Find
Meaning in Life without Drugs.

---

*When you do something, if you fix your mind on the activity with some
confidence, the quality of your state of mind is the activity itself.*
– Shunryu Suzuki, Zen Mind, Beginner Mind

INTRODUCTION

- Rewire the reward pathway with yoga nidra.
- Practice nonattachment.
- Disengage the craving impulse mindfully.
- Become aware of triggers.
- Lower stress through nonaction.
- Discover the deeper self.
- Engage in the world.

Overcoming dependence on a substance or any type of addiction such as gambling and sex addiction is a kind of negative meditation. The person who sincerely tries to give up these compelling habits is completely and deeply engaged. By subtly shifting this intense focus meditatively towards wholesome positive activities, withdrawal can become a meditative journey that leads to a far more enlightened life without depending on something external like drugs or gambling. Meditation works best when the therapist engages multiple levels within clients to help them conquer the pull of the addiction's powerful effects on mind and brain.

Meditation works directly on mind, brain, and body to help restore a more normal balance and better adjustment. And its regular practice can offer your clients a different perspective on their pleasure-seeking, pain-avoiding patterns. You can give them a tool to relieve their suffering that does not rely on something outside of themselves, such as drugs. And by practicing meditation regularly, they can rewire the connections in the brain and reward circuitry that tend to perpetuate drug use, making it easier for them to choose withdrawal, follow through without relapse, and develop new behavior patterns.

HOW SUBSTANCE ABUSE CHANGES THE BRAIN

The neuroscience theory of addiction explains why it can be so difficult to overcome an addictive habit because addictive behaviors alter the reward pathway of the brain. The reward pathway is found at the very center of the brain. (This was illustrated in Figure 11.1.)

People don't realize that we are wired to be happy. We seek pleasurable experiences, such as eating, sleeping, and having sex. When we engage in one of these activities, dopamine is released, correlating with a feeling of pleasure. The powerful experience of pleasure clients get from taking drugs is due to how drugs activate the reward pathway to release dopamine. The use of an addictive substance brings about a strong sense of pleasure as the substance enters the bloodstream and brain. Users feel an intense craving to repeat the experience. But when drugs are used regularly, the reward pathway becomes intertwined with the drug effect, such that clients may find little joy in anything but the drug.

Addictive behaviors such as gambling, sex addiction, and even self-cutting, also engage the reward pathway by releasing dopamine. Therefore, these kinds of problems can also be treated with the techniques included in this chapter.

Meditation helps to rewire the reward pathway back to normal. Certain yoga focus meditations cause a release of dopamine to help clients experience enjoyment without drugs, a first step in unlinking the connection between addiction and the reward pathway. Mindfulness meditation can help detach from cravings by altering the pleasure-pain struggle. In addition, meditation lowers the physical discomforts that accompany withdrawal. And through regular meditative practice, clients will rediscover their natural pleasure in life itself arising from their own inner resources.

REWIRE THE REWARD PATHWAY BY PRODUCING WELL-BEING MEDITATIVELY

People who abuse drugs or alcohol have depleted their dopamine, which explains why they often find most of life's pleasures uninteresting. Research on the focus meditation method known as *yoga nidra,* often defined as a state of deep relaxation, has been shown to increase dopamine release. A group of researchers in Denmark found that performing yoga nidra meditation increased the release of dopamine by 65% (Kjaer et al., 2002).

Exercise 19.1: Yoga Nidra Relaxation

Lie down on your back. If your back is sore, place a pillow under your legs behind the knees, which will relax the lower back. Breathe comfortably in and out for several minutes as you allow your breathing to relax. Now focus your attention on your right foot. Allow it to relax as completely as possible. Then move your attention up through your leg to your knee, relaxing these areas. Continue to move your attention all the way up to your thigh and then to your hip, relaxing all the muscles as you go. Now become aware of your entire leg, letting it relax completely. Next, move to your left foot and let your attention travel up to your hip, relaxing as you go. Now move up though your whole body, part by part, relaxing as you go. Notice your torso area, front and back, waist, chest, lower to middle to upper back, right hand, arm, shoulder, then left, until your attention is focused all the way up to your neck, throat, face, and finally the top of your head. When you have finished, breathe comfortably as you notice your entire body, relaxed and at ease. Finally, feel your body as it meets the surface you lie on, then extend your awareness to include the place where you are. When you feel ready, open your eyes and stretch. You will notice that you feel more relaxed and refreshed from your pleasurable focus meditation experience. Practice this meditation daily to help your nervous system regain its natural capacity to enjoy life of itself, without external stimulation from an outside substance.

A MINDFUL THEORY OF ADDICTION: BEYOND PLEASURE AND PAIN

Addiction is usually defined as the craving people feel that impels them to seek after a certain substance or experience. But this seeking for the substance is part of a far more pervasive general problem that is found in every area of life: the problem of desire in general. The real solution to addiction is to root out desire at its source: the endless cycle of seeking pleasure and avoiding pain. This seeking and avoiding will never lead to happiness, only to suffering, because all things, even the pleasurable ones, are impermanent. People can live free of addiction by developing mindfulness. From the calm, meditative center a new kind of happiness develops.

The first step in gaining a meditative center is to train mindfulness skills. Spend time during each session with your client simply observing, without judgment or change, when he or she feels comfortable and relaxed. Use the mindfulness exercises in Chapter 9. Be mindful of sensations, feelings, thoughts, and stay in the moment. Then, when your client is ready, you can direct his/her mindfulness to go beyond pleasure and pain.

Exercise 19.2: Warm Up to Nonattachment

The ability to go beyond pleasure and pain begins with nonattachment. Nonattachment can be practiced, at first, on small likes and dislikes, such as eating a food that you feel neutral about.

Pick a food you feel somewhat neutral about—perhaps one you don't mind and eat because you know it's good for you. When chewing, pay close attention to the taste, texture, and aroma. Note the qualities of the taste, without like or dislike. Simply be aware of the taste and accept them as they are. Repeat the experiment with a food you slightly dislike. Accept, while noticing the taste, texture, and aroma. Finally, test yourself by tasting a food you don't like at all while remaining neutral. The development of an accepting but disengaged attitude takes practice.

Exercise 19.3: Nonattachment to Cravings

When your client has developed some skill with nonattachment, encourage applying the skill to craving sensations.

When craving occurs, sit down and focus attention on it, not by thinking about how terrible it is but rather by applying nonattachment. Open your focus as you notice the sensations you are experiencing just as sensations. If you start to label them as negative, notice that and return a neutral observation of the full range experiencing that you feel. Let your breathing settle and your muscles relax while sitting quietly. Turn attention to breathing as well. While observing, allow any unnecessary tensions to ease. If the thoughts move away from the moment, gently bring them back. Continue to examine your craving as just a group of sensations. Stay with the feeling while allowing yourself to be aware of other sensations as well. Notice that the full range of your experience includes far more. Pleasures and pains come and go, so seek a neutral path between, calm, centered, and mindfully aware. The sensation changes in context.

Continue to breathe as comfortably as possible while observing. Usually the craving feeling will alter in various ways. Notice the changes as they occur. After a time, the sensations may even ease or diminish.

Exercise 19.4: Applying Open Focus to Identifying Triggers Mindfully

Therapy teaches clients about the people and places that tend to trigger their drug use. Mindfulness can help your clients to identify places where the craving is stimulated, people who are associated with it, and personal behaviors and thoughts that accompany it. Noticing mindfully will give your clients more freedom to choose. It is easier to take a different action when mindfulness is practiced, before being swept away by a reaction. The earlier the intervention, the easier it will be to make a different choice. This practice will require that the user stop to observe mindfully at many times through the day and evening, becoming aware of typical patterns. The exercise applies a pattern that is consistent throughout meditational therapy.

Take a mindful glance at random times as you go through your day. Notice what you sense, feel, and think as you interact with others and go to typical places. You may find that experiences you have had led you toward desiring your drug. Maintain the contemplative perspective. Now that you are developing awareness of yourself in the present moment, you may have times when you feel strongly that you can choose to turn away from using instead. At such moments, try to sense this experience of inner strength vividly. Contemplate the future that you are setting in motion, the new beginnings of your life, without using.

LOWER STRESS

Relaxing and calming in itself may help in overcoming addiction. Recent research shows that addicts may be more prone to stress than persons who are not addicted. Developing calm will offer some stress reduction and add confidence your clients need to take the next step to withdrawal. Use the meditations for stress in Chapter 13 along with the exercise that follows.

Exercise 19.5: Lower Stress through Nonaction

Here is a method for lowering stress that often appeals to substance abusers, the way of nonaction, known as *wuwei*. This meditation begins a process of stress reduction by not taking any deliberate action but instead simply letting nature take its course while following its path with awareness. Paradoxically, the person gains more self-control. *Wuwei* control works like steering the wheels of a car in the direction of a skid until the car is on track again. Then the car rights itself, and control becomes possible.

Sit quietly. Is it possible to permit your eyes to rest, or are they watching? Notice this but don't change it. Pay attention to breathing, but don't alter it. Simply allow it to be as it is. Scan through your body. Notice any tension, but don't try to force relaxation. Allow your muscles to be as they are. How does your body meet the floor if you are lying down (or chair if you are sitting)? Do you let the floor (or chair) support your body, or is your body pushing against the floor (or chair)? Notice these things. Personally significant patterns are often encoded implicitly in subtle experiences.

Next, turn attention to thoughts. Note any thoughts that occur, but don't attempt to direct them. Simply observe, allowing them to be as they are. Follow whatever awareness presents, but don't try to change. Be as you are. Does breathing become easier? Are your muscles relaxing of their own accord? Do you feel calmer? In noticing, without altering anything purposefully, change begins to take place, and stress levels will lower. Allow what is natural to find its own balance, as it inevitably will.

DISCOVER YOUR DEEPER NATURE

People involved in addiction often construe themselves as users, gamblers, etc. and have a hard time imagining themselves without this need. Often the sense of self is distorted, and this distortion may interfere with therapeutic progress. Identity becomes deeply intertwined with the addiction. Meditation can bring a grasp of a more unbiased and flexible sense of self. The enduring, fixed self is experienced in meditation as a flow that evolves and changes.

Exercise 19.6: Open Focus on This Moment: A New Identity without Drugs

Take a mindful breath, in and out. Then notice the next breath, a completely new breath. Each breath is a new breath, just as each moment is a new moment. If doubts or worries arise, notice them, but don't let them distract from what is occurring in this moment now. Meditate on the new, open moment. Whatever you have been before has passed. The next moment is a new moment, filled with potential.

As you sustain this quiet meditation for a few minutes, you will begin to feel a sense of self emerge that relies on nothing outside of yourself. Although thoughts, worries, and fears might interfere at times, moments of peace can also occur. The peaceful moments grow longer and your sense of peace grows stronger as you practice. Even a fleeting moment of quiet begins the process. Keep practicing and allowing your strong sense of self, based in the experience of calm clarity developed in meditation. Return to the open flow of your experiencing as it is unfolding. Keep coming back to this present moment, a fresh start.

Exercise 19.7: Engage in the World

Addictions draw people away from their engagement with the world of meaningful pursuits. They also lose touch with their true nature by narrowing down their lives. Encourage your clients to rediscover their interests and reclaim talents that they may not be expressing. By getting involved in activities, clients can help to free themselves to find reward and enjoyment in life itself as they express their deeper nature.

Sit quietly and reflect on your interests. What did you like to do as a child? What interests did you engage in before you got involved in your addiction? Once you have identified an interest or skill that you used to enjoy, vividly imagine yourself doing it now. Imaginatively gather any supplies you need. Think of yourself performing any preparations that are needed. Engage all of your senses: What do you feel, see, and sense as you start expressing this interest? Follow the action from start to finish. Imagine yourself doing it well. Stay with the activity for several minutes. Enjoy the experience! You have engaged the ideomotor response. With repeated practice over time, you initiate a process. Then, when you perform the activity in the world, the action will flow naturally and confidently.

CONCLUSION

Mindfulness helps you go beyond seeking pleasure and avoiding pain. Mindfulness can help clients to stabilize in the present moment, detach from the discomforts, and open to something new. When working on overcoming substance abuse, encourage them to meditate several times each day and to stay with it. This kind of personal work, when coupled with your professional care, can help your clients to master their addiction and attune to their real needs for fulfillment.

20

Conclusions

Core Principle 20: Sculpt Your Own Life through Regular Meditation as You Discover that Enlightened Well-being Is Here and Now.

Many of our clients go through their day intent on their purpose or embroiled in thought within, with less awareness of themselves in the moment. They often function on an implicit, unconscious level, out of touch with their deeper nature. Of course, simply facing a painful repressed memory may not be enough. But the practice of meditation provides a gently powerful set of techniques that fosters awareness, so that even the most disturbing experiences can be noticed, accepted, and worked through. In this sense, meditation for therapy is more than a set of techniques: It is a path for clients to take a hand in their own healing process. It adds clarity of vision that is receptive while also being objective. It strengthens the capacity to tolerate discomfort and accept it as it is without making it worse. And it opens the client to feelings of joy, fulfillment, and well-being that they may not have experienced for a long time.

Meditative lessons are simple yet profound: Life can be lived fully when you are immersed in each moment. Through the practice of meditation, everything becomes an opportunity to become more awake and aware. And you can be happy, here and now. Meditation inspires and uplifts even the most downtrodden soul to find peace within and with the greater world.

We leave you with a meditation for you and your client to practice any time each day. Using the built-in abilities you have to focus, open focus, and let go of focus can attune you to yourself and your world at any given moment. Stay on your path, guiding and inspiring your clients. Your clients will glow with the healing spirit you skillfully and compassionately communicate to them.

Exercise 20.1 Grounding in the Moment

At various times during the day, whenever you can, take a moment to stop and focus attention on where you are and what you are doing. Look around, hear the sounds, notice the smells, and feel the ground beneath your feet or chair that supports you as you sit. Next, open your focus to your moment-to-moment experience. Notice each breath in and out, following the shifting flow of your thoughts, feelings, and sensations moment by moment. Finally, sit or stand quietly as you clear your mind of all thought, without focusing on anything in particular. Be present in the moment now.

Get in touch in this way as often as you can. In time, you will feel naturally attuned, in balance with yourself and your surroundings, accepting the flow of your life as it goes. Take a quick meditative glance and do it regularly. Stay with each moment anew. Your future path will become an open path. Return to the present moment. Free yourself of the past. An uncharted future lies ahead. Release your potential, which is just waiting to be expressed.

References

Abela, J. R. Z., & D'Alessandro, D. U. (2002). Beck's cognitive theory of depression: A test of the diathesis-stress and causal mediation components. *British Journal of Clinical Psychology, 41,* 111–128.

Abou-Nader, T. M., Alexander, C. N., & Davies, J. L. (1990). The Maharishi technology of the unified field and reduction of armed conflict: A comparative longitudinal study of Lebanese villages. In R. A. Chalmers, C. Clements, H. Schenkluhn, & M. Weinless (Eds.), *Scientific research in the Transcendental Meditation and TM-Sidhi program: Collected papers* (Vol. 4, 2623–2633). Vlodrop, Netherlands: Maharishi Vedic University Press.

Adler, K. A., & Deutsch, D. (Eds.). (1959). *Essays in individual psychology: Contemporary applications of Alfred Adler's theories.* New York, NY: Grove Press.

Alexander, C. N., Rainforth M. V., & Gelderloos, P. (1991). Transcendental meditation, self-actualization, and psychological health: A conceptual overview and statistical meta-analysis. *Journal of Social Behavior and Personality, 6*(5), 189–248.

Altman, D. (2014). *The mindfulness toolbox: 50 practical tips, tools, & handouts for anxiety, depression, stress, and pain.* Eau Claire, WI: PESI Publishig and Media.

American Psychological Association. (2008, October 7). Stress in America: Mind/body health: For a healthy mind and body, talk to a psychologist. Washington DC: American Psychological Association.

Aristotle. (2008). *Physics*. Oxford, UK: Oxford University Press.

Badawi, K., Wallace, R. K., Orme-Johnson, D., & Rouzere, A. M. (1984). Electrophysiologic characteristics of reparatory suspension periods occurring during the practice of the transcendental meditation program. *Psychosomatic Medicine, 46*(3), 267–276.

Bhatia, M., Kumar, A., Kumar, N., Pandey, R. M., & Kochupilla, V. (2003). Electrophysiologic evaluation of Sudarshan Kriaya: An EEG, BAER and P300 study. *Indian Journal of Pharmacology, 47*, 157–163.

Boyke, J., Driemeyer, J., Gaser, C., Buchel, C., & May, A. (2008). Training-induced brain structure changes in the elderly. *Journal of Neuroscience, 28*, 7031–7033.

Braboszcz, C., Habnusseau, S., & Delorme, A. (2010). Meditation and neuroscience: From basic research to clinical practice. In R. Carlstedt (Ed.), *Integrating psychology, psychiatry, and behavioral medicine. Perspectives, practices, and research*. New York, NY: Springer.

Breedlove, S. M., Rosenzweig, M. R., & Watson, N. V. (2007). *Biological psychology: An introduction to behavioral, cognitive, and clinical neuroscience*. Sunderland, MA: Sinauer Associates.

Brown, K. W., Goodman, R. J., & Inzlicht, M. (2013, January 8). Dispositional mindfulness and the attenuation of neural responses to emotional stimuli. *Social Cognitive and Affective Neuroscience, 8*(1), 93–99. doi: 10.1093/scan/nss004

Brown, K. W., & Ryan, R. M. (2003). The benefits of being present: Mindfulness and its role in psychological well-being. *Journal of Personality and Social Psychology, 84*(4), 822–848.

Buddha. (1996). *Mahasatipatthana Sutta: The great discourse on the establishment of awareness*. Maharashtra, India: Vipassana Research Institute.

Cahn, R., Delome, A., & Polich, J. (2010). Occipital gamma activation during Vipassana meditation. *Cognitive Processing, 11*(1), 39–56.

Chan, W. T. (1963). *A sourcebook in Chinese philosophy*. Princeton, NJ: Princeton University Press.

Conze, E. (1995). *Buddhist texts through the ages*. Oxford: Oneworld Publications.

Craig, A. D. (2002). How do you feel? Interoception: The sense of the physiological condition of the body. *Nature Reviews, Neuroscience, 3*, 655–666.

Craig, A. D. (2009). How do you feel now? The anterior insula and human awareness. *Nature Reviews, Neuroscience, 10*, 59–70.

Creswell, J. D., Way, B. M., Eisenberger, N. I., & Lieberman, M. D. (2007). Neural correlates of dispositional mindfulness during affect labeling. *Psychosomatic Medicine, 69*, 560–565.

Dalai Lama & Cutler, H. C. (1998). *The art of happiness*. Norwalk, CT: Eaton Press.

Dantzker J. M. (2006) Bursting on the scene: How thalamic neurons grab your attention. *PLOS Biology, 4*(7), e250.

Derntl, B., Seidel, E. M., Kryspin-Exner, I., Hasmann, A., & Dobmeier, M. (2009). Facial emotion recognition in patients with bipolar I and bipolar II disorder. *British Journal of Clinical Psychology, 48*(4), 363–375.

Desbordes, G., Negi, L. T., Pace, T., Wallace, B. A., Raison, C. L., & Schwartz, E. L. (2012). Effects of mindful-attention and compassion meditation training on amygdala response to emotional stimuli in an ordinary, non-meditative state. *Frontiers in Human Neuroscience, 6*, 292. doi:10.3389/fnhum.2012.00292

Dhar, H. L. (2002). Meditation, health, intelligence and performance. *Medicine Update APICON, 202*, 1376–1379.

Dillbeck, M. C., & Orme-Johnson, D. W. (1987). Physiological differences between transcendental meditation and rest. *American Psychologist, 42*(9), 879–881.

Druppa, Gyalwa Gendun. (1993). *Training the mind in the great way*. Ithaca, NY: Snow Lion.

Duyvendak, J. J. L. (1992). *Tao Te Ching, The book of the way and its virtue*. Boston, MA: Tuttle.

Emmons, R. A., & McCullough, M. E. (2003). Counting blessings versus burdens: An experimental investigation of gratitude and subjective well-being in daily life. *Journal of Personality and Social Psychology, 84*(2), 377–389.

Francis, D. D., Szegda, K., Campbell, G., Martin, W. D., & Insel, T. R. (2003). Epigenetic sources of behavioral differences in mice. *Nature Neuroscience, 6*(5), 445–446.

Frank, J. D., & Frank, J. (1991). *Persuasion and healing*. Baltimore, MD: Johns Hopkins University Press.

Frank, J. D., Hoehn-Saric, R., Imber, S., Liberman, B., & Stone, A. (1978). *Effective ingredients of successful psychotherapy.* New York, NY: Brunner/Mazel.

Fredrickson, B. L., & Branigan, C. (2005). Positive emotions broaden the scope of attention and thought-action repertoires. *Cognition & Emotion, 19,* 313–332.

Gage, F. H., Eriksson, P. S., Perfilieva, E., & Bjork-Eriksson, T. (1998). Neurogenesis in the adult human hippocampus. *Nature Medicine, 4*(11), 1313–1317.

Garland, E. L., Fredrickson, B., Kring, A. M., Johnson, D. P., Meyer, P. S., & Penn, D. L. (2010) Upward spirals of positive emotions counter downward spirals of negativity: Insights from the broaden-and-build theory and affective neuroscience on the treatment of emotion dysfunctions and deficits in psychopathology. *Clinical Psychology Review, 30,* 849–864.

Granath, J., Ingvarsson, S., von Thiele, U., & Lundberg, U. (2006). Stress management: A randomized study of cognitive behavioral therapy and yoga therapy. *Cognitive Behavior Therapy, 35*(1), 3–10.

Grant, J. A., & Rainville, P. (2009). Pain sensitivity and analgesic effects of mindful states in Zen meditators: A cross-sectional study. *Psychosomatic Medicine, 71*(1), 106–114. doi:10.1097/psy.0b013e31818f52ee

Grant, J. A., Courtemanche, J., & Rainville, P. (2011). A non-elaborative mental stance and decoupling of executive and pain-related cortices predicts low pain sensitivity in Zen meditators. *Pain, 152*(1), 150–156. doi:10.1016/j.pain.2010.10.006

Grossman, P., Niemann, L., Schmidt, S., & Walach, H. (2004). Mindfulness-based stress reduction and health benefits: A meta-analysis. *Journal of Psychosomatic Research, 57*(1), 35–43.

Hankey, A. (2006). Studies of advanced stages of meditation in the Tibetan Buddhist and Vedic traditions. 1: A comparison of general changes. *Evidence Based Complementary Alternative Medicine, 3*(4), 513–521.

Hotzel, B. K., Carmody, J., Vangel, M., Congleton, C., Yarramsetti, S. M., Gard, T., & Lazar, S. W. (2011). Mindfulness practice leads to increases in regional brain gray matter density. *Psychiatry Research: Neuroimaging, 191*(1), 36–43.

Hubble, M. A., Duncan, B. L., & Miller, S. D. (2000). *The heart and soul of change: What works in therapy*. Washington, DC: American Psychological Association.

Hugdahl, K. (1996). Cognitive influences on human autonomic nervous system function. *Current Opinion in Neurobiology, 6*, 252–258.

Jacobson, E. (1929). *Progressive relaxation*. Chicago, IL: University of Chicago Press.

Jacobson, E. (1934) *You must relax*. New York, NY: Whittlesey House.

James, W. (1896). *The principles of psychology in two volumes*. New York, NY: Holt.

Jensen, O., Kaiser, J., & Lachaux, J. P. (2007). Human gamma-frequency oscillations associated with attention and memory. *Trends in Neurosciences, 30*(7), 317–324.

Jerath, R., Edry, J. W., Bames, V. A., & Jerath, V. (2006). Physiology of long pranayamic breathing: Neural respiratory elements may provide a mechanism that explains how slow deep breathing shifts the autonomic nervous system. *Medical Hypotheses, 67*(3), 556–571.

Kabat-Zinn, J. (2003). *Coming to our senses: Healing ourselves and the world through mindfulness*. New York, NY: Hyperion.

Kabat-Zinn, J. (2013). *Full catastrophe living: Using the wisdom of your body and mind to face stress, pain, and illness*. New York, NY: Bantam Books.

Kabat-Zinn, J., Massion, M. D., Dristeller, J., Peterson, L. G., Fletcher, K. E., Pbert, L. et.al. (1992) Effectiveness of a mindfulness-based stress reduction program in the treatment of anxiety disorders. *American Journal of Psychiatry, 149*, 936–943.

Kendler, K. S., Liu, X. Q., Gardner, C. O., McCullough, M. E., Larson, D., & Prescott, C. A. (2003). Dimensions of religiosity and their relationship to lifetime psychiatric and substance use disorders. *American Journal of Psychiatry, 160*, 496–503.

Kheirbek, M. A., & Hen, R. (2011). Dorsal VS ventral hippocampal neurogenesis: Implications for cognition and mood. *Neuropsychopharmacology, 36*, 373–374.

Kjaer, T. W., Bertelsen, C., Piccini, P., Brooks, D. Alving, J. & Lou, H. C. (2002). Increased dopamine tone during meditation-induced change of consciousness. *Brain Research: Cognitive Brain Research, 13*(2), 255–259.

Kohr. R. L. (1977). Dimensionality in the meditative experience. *Journal of Transpersonal Psychology, 9*(2), 193–203.

Korunka, C., Tement, S., Zdrehus, C., & Borza, A. (2010). Burnout: Definition, recognition and prevention approaches. In *BOIT: Burnout intervention training for managers and team leaders.*

Lang, P. J. (1994). The Varieties of Emotional Experience: A Meditation on James-Lange Theory. *Psychological Review, 101,* 211–221.

Langer, E. J. (1989). *Mindfulness.* Cambridge, MA: Da Capo Press.

Lazar, S. W., Kerr, C. E., Wasserman, R. H., Gray, J. R., Greve, M., Treadway, T., … Fishi, B. (2005). Meditation experience is associated with increased cortical thickness. *NeuroReport, 16*(17), 1893–1897.

Lee, M. S., Kang, C. W., Lim, H. J., & Lee. M. S. (2004) Effects of Qi-training on anxiety and plasma concentrations of cortisol, ACTH and aldosterone: A randomized placebo-controlled pilot study. *Stress and Health, 20*(5), 243–248.

Legge, J. (1962). *The texts of Taoism.* New York, NY: Dover.

Lembke, A., & Ketter, T. A. (2002). Impaired recognition of facial emotion in mania. *American Journal of Psychiatry, 159,* 302–304.

LoLordo, V. M., & Overmier, J. B. (2011). Trauma, learned helplessness, its neuroscience, and implications for posttraumatic stress disorder. In T. R. Schachtman & S. S. Reilly, *Associative learning and conditioning theory: Human and nonhuman applications.* London, UK: Oxford University Press.

Low, A. (2000). *Zen and the sutras.* Boston, MA: Tuttle.

Lutz, A., Brefczynski-Lewis, J., Johnstone, T., & Davidson, R. J. (2008a). Regulation of the neural circuitry of emotion by compassion meditation: Effects of meditative expertise. *PLOS One, 3*(3), e1897. doi:10.1371/journal.pone.0001897

Lutz, A., Gretschar, L. L., Rawlings, N., Ricard, M., & Davidson, R. J. (2004). Long-term meditators self-induce high-amplitude gamma synchrony during mental practice. *Neuroscience, 101*(46), 16369–16373.

Lutz, A., Slagter, H. A., Dunne, J. D., & Davidson, R. J. (2008b). Attention regulation and monitoring in meditation. *Trends in Cognitive Sciences, 12*(4), 163-9.

MacLean, P. D. (1985). Brain evolution relating to family, play and the separation call. *Archives of General Psychiatry, 42,* 405–417.

Maguire, E. A., Gadian, D. G., Johnsrude, I. S., Good, C. D., Ashburner, J., Frackowiak, R. S. J., & Frith, C. D. (2000). Navigation related structural change in the hippocampi of taxi drivers. *Proccedings of the National Academy of Sciences, 97*(8), 4398–4403.

Meaney, M. J. (2001). Maternal care, gene expression, and the transmission of individual differences in stress reactivity across generations. *Annual Review of Neuroscience, 24,* 1161–1192.

Meichenbaum, D. (2012). *Roadmap to resilience: A guide for military, trauma victims and their families.* Miami, FL: Institute Press.

Moruzzi, G., & Magoun, H. W. (1959). Brain stem reticular formation and activation of EEG. *Electroencephalography and Clinical Neurophysiology, 1,* 455–473.

Mullin, G. H. (1982). *The path to enlightenment: H.H. the Dalai Lama.* Ithaca, New York, NY: Snow Lion.

Murray, G., & Johnson, S. L. (2010). The clinical significance of creativity in bipolar disorder. *Clinical Psychology Review, 30,* 721–732.

Musashi, M. (1974). *The book of five rings.* New York, NY: Overland Press.

Pagnoni, G., Cekic, M., & Guo, Y. (2008). "Thinking about not-thinking": Neural correlates of conceptual processing during Zen meditation. *PLOS One, 3*(9), e3083. doi:10.1371/journal.pone.0003083

Patanjali. (n.d.). *The Yoga Sutras of Patanjali: The threads of union* (BonGiovanni, Trans.). Available at www.sacred-texts.com/hin/yogasutr.htm

Paulus, M. P., & Stein, M. B. (2006). An insular view of anxiety. *Biological Psychiatry, 60,* 383–387.

Payne, P., & Crane-Godreau, M. A. (2013). Meditative movement for depression and anxiety. *Frontiers in Psychiatry, 4,* 71.

Perls, F. (1969). *Gestalt therapy verbatim.* Lafayette, CA: Real People Press.

Plato. (1892). *The dialogues of Plato* (3rd ed., Vol. 1). Translated by B. Jowett. London, UK: Oxford University Press.

Porges, S. W. (2011). *The polyvagal theory: Neurophysiological foundations of emotions, attachment, communication, self-regulation.* New York, NY: Norton.

Posner, M. I., Rothbart, M. K., Sheese, B. F., & Tang, Y. (2007). The anterior cingulate gyrus and the mechanisms of self-regulation. *Cognitive, Affective, and Behavioral Neuroscience, 7*(4), 391–395.

Price, A. F., & Mou-lam, W. (1990). *The Diamond Sutra and the sutra of Hui-Neng*. Boston, MA: Shambala Books.

Rausch, S. M., Gramling, S. E., & Auerbach, S. M. (2006). Effects of a single session of large-group meditation and progressive muscle relaxation training on stress reduction, reactivity, and recovery. *International Journal of Stress Management, 13*(3), 273–290.

Ross, N. W. (1960). *The world of Zen: An East-West anthology*. New York, NY: Vintage Books.

Rossi, E. L. (2002). *The psychobiology of gene expression: Neuroscience and neurogenesis in hypnosis and the healing arts*. New York, NY: Norton.

Sala, M., Perez, J., Soloff, P., Ucelli di Nemi, S., Caverzase, E., Soares, J. C., & Brambillia, P. (2004). Stress and hippocampal abnormatlities in psychiatric disorders. *European Journal of Neuropsychopharmacology, 14*(5), 393–406.

Seligman, M. E. P., Steen, T. A., Park, N., & Peterson, C. (2005). Positive psychology progress: Empirical validation of interventions. *American Psychologist, 60*, 410–421.

Simpkins, C. A., & Simpkins, A. M. (2009). *Meditation for therapists and their clients*. New York, NY: Norton.

Simpkins, C. A., & Simpkins, A. M. (2010a). *The Dao of neuroscience*. New York, NY: Norton.

Simpkins, C. A., & Simpkins, A. M. (2010b). *Meditation and yoga in psychotherapy: Techniques for clinical practice*. Hoboken, NJ: Wiley.

Simpkins, C. A., & Simpkins, A. M. (2011). *Zen meditation in psychotherapy: Techniques for clinical practice*. Hoboken, NJ: Wiley.

Simpkins, C. A., & Simpkins, A. M. (2012). *Neuroscience for clinicians*. New York, NY: Springer.

Slagter, H. A., Lutz, A., Greischar, L. L., Francis, A. D., Nieuwenhuis, S., Davis, J. M., & Davidson, R. J. (2007). Mental training affects distribution of limited brain resources. *PLOS Biology, 5*, e138.

Spear, L. (2010). *The behavioral neuroscience of adolescence*. New York, NY: Norton.

Strakowski, S. M., DelBello, M. P., Sax, K. W., Zimmerman, M. E., Shear, P. K., Hawkins, J. M., & Larson, E. R. (1999). Brain magnetic resonance imaging of structural abnormalities in bipolar disorder. *Archives of General Psychiatry, 56*, 254–260.

Suzuki, D. T. (1969). *The Zen doctrine of no-mind*. York Beach, ME: Samuel Weiser.

Suzuki, S. (1979). *Zen mind, beginner mind*. New York, NY: Weatherhill.

Tang, Y.-Y., Lu, Q., Geng, X., Stein, E. A., Yang, Y., & Posner, M. I. (2010). Short-term meditation induces white matter changes in the anterior cingulate. *Proceedings of the National Academy of Sciences, 107*(35), 15649–15652.

Tang, Y.-Y., Ma, Y., Fan, Y.., Feng, H., Wang, J., Feng, S., ... Fan, M. (2009). Central and autonomic nervous system interaction is altered by short-term meditation. *Proceedings of the National Academy of Sciences, 106*(22), 8865–8870.

Travis, F., & Shear, J. (2010). Focused attention, open monitoring and automatic self-transcending: Categories to organize meditations from Vedic, Buddhist and Chinese traditions. *Consciousness and Cognition, 19*, 1110–1119.

Vallée, M., Mayo, W., Dellu, F., Le Moal, M., Simon, H., & Maccari, S. (1997). Prenatal stress induces high anxiety and postnatal handling induces low anxiety in adult offspring: Correlations with stress-induced corticosterone secretion. *Journal of Neuroscience, 17*(7), 2626–2636.

Vaitl, D., & Ott, U. (2005). Altered states of consciousness induced by psychophysiological techniques. *Mind and Matter, 3*, 9–30.

Vivekananda. (1953). *The yogas and other works*. New York, NY: Ramakrishna-Vivekananda Center.

Wallace, B. A., & Shapiro, S. L. (2006). Mental balance and well-being: Building bridges between Buddhism and Western psychology. *American Psychologist, 61*(7), 690–701.

Watson, B. (1968). *The complete works of Chuang Tzu*. New York, NY: Columbia University Press.

Wilhelm, H., & Wilhelm, R. (1995). *Understanding the i ching*. Princeton, NJ: Princeton University Press.

Wood, A. M., Froh, J. J., & Geraghty, A. (2010). Gratitude and well-being: A review and theoretical integration. *Clinical Psychology Review, 30*(7), 890–905. doi:10.1016/j.cpr.2010.03.005

Yang, K. H., Kim, Y. H., & Lee, M. S. (2005). Efficacy of Qi-therapy (external Qigong) for elderly people with chronic pain. *International Journal of Neuroscience, 115*(7), 949–963.

Yutang, L. (1942). *The wisdom of China and India*. New York, NY: Random House.

Zahn, R., Moll, J., Paiva, M., Garrido, G., Krueger, F., Huey, E. D., & Grafman, J. (2009). The neural basis of human social values: evidence from functional MRI. *Cerebral Cortex, 19*(2), 276–283.

Zehr, J. L., Todd, B. J., Schultz, K. M., McCarthy, M. M., & Sisk, C. L. (2006). Dendrite pruning of the medial amygdala during pubertal development of the male Syrian hamster. *Journal of Neurobiology, 66*, 578–590.

Zhang, Y., Chen, Y., Bressler, S. L., & Ding, M. (2008). Response preparation and inhibition: The role of the cortical sensorimotor beta rhythm. *Neuroscience, 156*(1), 238–246.

Zillmer, E. R., Spiers, M. V., & Culbertson, W. C. (2008). *Principles of neuropsychology*. Belmont, CA: Thomson Wadsworth.

About the Authors

C. Alexander Simpkins, PhD, and Annellen M. Simpkins, PhD, are psychologists specializing in meditation, hypnotherapy, and neuroscience. The Simpkinses are authors of 28 books, many of them bestsellers. Some of their most recent titles are: *The Yoga and Mindfulness Therapy Workbook* (PESI, 2014), *The Tao of Bipolar: Using Meditation and Mindfulness to Find Balance and Peace* (New Harbinger, 2013), *Neuroscience for Clinicians* (Springer, 2012), *Zen Meditation in Psychotherapy* (Wiley, 2011), *Meditation and Yoga in Psychotherapy: Techniques for Clinical Practice* (Wiley, 2010), *The Dao of Neuroscience* (Norton, 2010), *Meditation for Therapists and Their Clients* (Norton, 2009), and *Neuro-Hypnosis* (Norton, 2010). *Resistance, Rebellion, and Growth* is forthcoming (Springer, 2016). Their books have more than 20 foreign editions and have won numerous awards.

The Simpkinses present seminars and workshops to professional audiences on the topics of yoga, mindfulness, meditation, neuroscience, and hypnosis for continuing education credits all around the world. They are invited speakers at professional conferences, state mental hospitals, and university campuses. They speak to popular audiences and have appeared on radio programs throughout the United States and Canada.

The Simpkinses have been practicing psychotherapy for more than four decades and have taught their meditative and hypnotic methods to facilitate mind-brain change in people of all ages. They have been involved in neuroscience for more than 20 years and teach Tae Chun Do, a martial art that includes yoga mindfulness, meditation, and breathing to address mind, body, and spirit. They have performed psychotherapy research and studied personally with psychotherapy masters, including Milton H. Erickson, Jerome D. Frank, Carl Rogers, Lawrence Kubie, and Ernest Rossi and with neuroscience experts Vilayanur Ramachandran, Jaime Pineda, Stephen Anagnostaras, and Paul Churchland. Their Eastern philosophy influence along with their commitment to continual learning and therapeutic effectiveness has helped them to look at things through the crystal of a unique vision, which they bring to you with warmth and clarity in their books and seminars.

Author Index

Subject Index

Page references followed by *fig* indicate an illustrated figure.

N